MUD, DAISIES'AND SPARROWS

Exploring outdoor environments

MUD, DAISIES' AND SPARROWS

Exploring outdoor environments

Dawn Anderson Brian McQuillen

NEW PRIMARY IDEAS

First published in Australia by Primary Education
Pty Ltd. in 1979.

Published in Great Britain by Studies in
Education Ltd. in 1980.

© Dawn Anderson, Brian McQuillen

Printed in Great Britain by Cheshire Typesetters Ltd.
Chester.

ISBN 090 5484 223
£3.25

Contents

Introduction

This book provides a guideline or model for language activities developing from a particular interest or theme. For example, *Exploring Outside Environments*.

The children use discovery methods, talk and play out their experiences and through art, photography, mathematics, science, constructions, music, drama and writing are involved in a total language approach. A language experience approach to reading can be developed by using children's recorded and written work.

The activities are meant to help children express themselves confidently with individuality, novelty and freshness. Personal exploration of ideas should reflect the curiosity and dynamic vitality of their emotions or feelings. The teacher should anticipate expression that is imaginative, sensitive, versatile and original.

Educators have long been advocating relating classroom activities to the children's own experiences and have stressed the significance of the children's spoken language competency to their overall language development. In 1951 Ruth Strickland[1] recommended an experience and language based curriculum. She did not consider language to be an academic subject but a medium to be enlarged through experience in its use. Andrew Wilkinson[2] has insisted that *oracy* should have a pre-eminent place in schools. In an early publication, Wilkinson summarised the main factors involved:

a) Speech and personality are one. To develop oracy one basically develops personality.

b) Language experience is crucial. Young children's use of language precedes their understanding of it (and this has implications for all the language learning).

c) The quality of language experience is crucial; quantity, though necessary, is not enough. The wrong language experience may result in a culturally induced backwardness.

d) Formal education by its stress on literacy has often been inimical to oracy. A synthesis is needed.

e) The national self-image has not encouraged oracy.

Teachers must value children's spoken language and they must refine and expand it for this, mostly informal, language will form the basis for all other language growth. We try to emphasise spoken language situations throughout the book.

Language must be seen as an operational tool learnt through constant use. When children share experiences with others they use language to build their own representational world. Direct experiences provide opportunities for learning through touch, taste, smell, sound and sight. The children, through their senses, will discriminate, sort and order their environment. They should discover something new and fresh in the familiar. They should be led to plunge into exploration and invention in an endeavour to understand natural connections and to draw inferences from their observations. A tree, waterfall, cave, bird or sand could be the starting point for discussion and experimentation, and this must go across all the subject areas.

The teacher strategies outlined in *Mud, Daisies and Sparrows* uses 'guided' discovery methods. The teacher structures the learning situation, drops hints and otherwise nudges the children to the brink of discovery. When a child already has adequate background knowledge, reception learning from a book or teacher explanation is seen to be quite defensible and more economical than the more time consuming discovery approach. We try not to put the children in situations where they are expected to learn through pure discovery methods. We expect the teacher to help the children find meaning.

Language across the curriculum need not be jargon. Examine your teacher style and attitudes and make the children's learning experiences full of warm, rich, exciting language that will help them find new understandings.

References

[1] R.G. Strickland, *The Language Arts in the Elementary School*, Heath & Co., Boston, 1951.

[2] A.M. Wilkinson (with contributions by A. Davies and D. Atkinson) 'Spoken English' *Educational Review*, Occasional Publications No. 2, supplement to Vol. 17, No. 2, February 1965.

Perception

Learning to use the senses more fully is crucial to enquiry methods of learning. All teachers know about the hierarchy of skills involved in the examination of the world around us. It is possible to talk about measuring, observing, classifying, predicting, inferring, hypothesising and experimenting without grasping the essential fact that all these skills need an understanding teacher to de-ritualise them and make sure that the children's initial interest is not lost in the formal processing of information. Any experience is likely to add to prior knowledge and understanding. It is the teacher's responsibility to acknowledge and respect what children already know and to use that knowledge as a springboard for future learning.

How effectively do children look, listen, touch, smell and taste? How well does the teacher assist the children to discriminate and compare? Teachers must organise their classrooms so that talk between partners or in small groups is possible. Each teacher must assist the children to find the focal points of subjects and utilise a variety of questioning techniques for the children's guidance. Use questions for finding specific information i.e. one answer is applicable; questions allowing the children to consider more than one explanation; questions considering situations not immediate to the actual matter being discussed. *What would happen if?* Also questions that begin to examine feelings and senses. *How does it feel? What would you do if?* The teacher can show the children how to examine an object in many ways:

What is its shape?
How many colours can you see?
Are there any patterns?
What kind of texture is it?
Is it heavy or light?
Can you see through it?
How many similar things can you find?
Would you roll it, throw it, push it or pull it?
Would you be able to use it in any other way?
How does it feel to hold it?
If it belonged to you would you give it away?

The teacher must increase the children's understanding of the object. It is real; can be seen, felt and moved. The object has properties of texture, shape, size, weight and colour. Through questioning, the children can be led to observe and understand these properties.

See if the children really understand what is meant by 'object'. Discuss and name things seen in the classroom. Handle some and ask the children to describe them in their own words. As a teacher, you should listen and be able to gauge the depth of the children's understanding of the properties of shape, size, texture, weight and colour observed in the object. Make your own contribution as an interested supportive person who wants to share the children's discoveries of dimensions additional to the original basic definition of the object.

Play games to assist the children's development of their senses. Here are some suggestions:

Blindfold Touch

The children are blindfolded and given an object to hold. Each child must describe the object and give its name using the senses of touching, smelling and hearing. Remove the blindfolds and see what other important properties the object has.

Working in pairs, one child is blindfolded and led around the room. The seeing partner presents objects and asks questions. The partners then reverse roles.

Another activity involves children working in small groups. All are blindfolded and objects are passed around with each child making a statement about the objects. The children are not to guess the actual name of any object. They are to state something about its properties using their five senses.

'Feelie' Bag

Have a bag full of interesting and diverse objects. Working in groups, each child dips into the bag without looking and describes an object fully before taking it out of the bag. Other children in the group can make guesses about the object from the information being given by the 'feeler'.

Hunt the Object

Prepare some cards with a description of the object *The object is flat and soft. It makes very little noise if you drop it on the floor. If you hit it with your hand something within it moves and floats in the air.* The children work in pairs, with those who are 'finders' asking their partners for additional clues if they are in trouble. The clues must only be about the object's properties.

Remember when choosing objects that you wish to increase the children's sensory awareness so select objects that can be heard, smelt, tasted and felt as well as those that can be touched.

Grouping Activities

Children are very interested in grouping collections of objects. Have some activities involving classification where they are able to sort objects with similar properties.

1 Provide the children with a box of objects for sorting. Ask them to group the objects having some sameness. Move amongst the children looking for those who might need your individual support. Talk with the less confident to encourage them. Find out why the children have grouped the objects in a particular way. Sometimes the selection of objects is based on some characteristic not obvious to the observer. Encourage the children to discuss their grouping with others. Challenge them sometimes to justify their classification.

2 Ask the children to supplement the sorting box with small objects from home so that there can be a greater range of groupings. Let them group the objects and explain why, then ask them to sort the objects into different groups for other reasons and explain why.

3 Build up a chart of words or pictures used to describe properties of objects. For younger children illustrate only one property on each chart e.g. *cold objects.*

4 Place on a flat surface a large collection of objects, sorting trays and captions (property words). The children sort the objects into trays labelled, for example, *sticky, fluffy, rough, shiny, stretchy, smooth, woolly.*

Individual children can participate in all these activities but make sure that communication between the child and others is encouraged. Through these carefully structured classroom activities children will gain understanding that will help them in their observations of the outside world.

When examining an outdoors environment, children have certain basic concepts about living things. *Living things are all around us; have basic requirements; change; have unique characteristics; provide many of humanity's basic requirements.*

Accepting the knowledge of such basic concepts, the teacher must provide a variety of experiences with many of the environmental materials to lead to a growth in understanding of these concepts. An 'outdoors education activity' (simple group work at school, a short or long excursion, a school camp) can provide the children with a chance to apply present knowledge and make new discoveries. Science and mathematics guides are full of suitable activities to act as starting points.

Remind the children to be careful of the natural environment.

They can examine their own school in a number of ways:

1 Assess the weathering effects on brick or stone work. Is it stained or clean?
2 Examine the angles of brick or stone. Are they sharp or rounded?
3 Look at the mortar between the bricks. Is it firm or crumbling?
4 Feel the building surface. Is it pitted or smooth?
5 Examine the woodwork, paint, metal and fabric fittings. In what condition are they?

In the school ground they can compare damp, shaded areas with dry, sunlit areas. Windy, open areas with sheltered, enclosed areas. These areas could provide insight into conditions affecting plant growth. See if they can discover why plants, moss and weeds grow where they do. Can they find out how the growth came to be there?

Take the children to a vacant lot near the school and divide the class into teams of three or five. These teams can stake out study plots of one or two square metres. Each team will list the litter found in their area and determine what effect this litter is having on plant and animal life. Does the litter encourage or discourage growth of plants or animals?

Teams can look for signs of animal life—burrows, tracks, droppings, feathers or hair. What kind of animals live there?

The teams list the kinds of plant life found in their plots. The children can develop their own key for all teams to locate these plants in their plots.

In the classroom draw a large map of the vacant block and list the most prominent types of plant life found there. Encourage the children to discuss why certain plants live where they are found. Why are there differences in plant life? Are certain animals to be found around particular plants?

The children can study their own home surroundings in a similar way and the three areas (school ground, vacant block and home surroundings) can be discussed and compared.

After outdoor excursions, try these experiments:

☐ Scrape soil from the children's shoes and place it on moist sand in a trough or tray. Keep the sand moist to germinate any seeds that may have been in the soil.

☐ Take a selection of seeds from plants found in a home garden (or use commercial packet seeds) and see how important the soil is to growth. Plant seeds in several different materials (clay, sand, compost) and at different depths (1 cm, 2 cm, 3 cm, 10 cm).

☐ See what effect water has on plants. Vary the amount from much to little to none. Use plastic bags or glass bottles over plants to see what effect this has.

☐ Set up particle collection devices. For example, leave a large piece of cloth in a corner of the room. Leave it for some weeks. Shake out everything that has gathered on it and place on moist sand. See if seeds in the cloth will germinate.

☐ Take soil from different areas and try to germinate the contained seeds. Use soil from various conditions such as damp shade; damp light; dry shade; dry light. Find out if different types of plants germinate in these conditions.

The asphalt playground provides opportunities to study water flow and evaporation. Compare the results of putting similar amounts of water on

a bare soil area with a hard surface
a freshly dug area
an asphalt area
an area of vegetation

Look at the street gutters and any drainage area in the school ground to observe water movement and any associated sounds. See if any silt has been deposited. Roof gutterings, downpipes and water drips provide experience with the changes in the environment as a result of the energy contained in running water. Often roof gutters become blocked by soil and plants can be found and examined. Cracks in the asphalt playground, the footpath and the gutters can be examined to see if any differences occur as to the number and types of plants found there.

Visits to natural settings should follow after the children have developed an environmental consciousness about their usual surroundings. They will have become aware of the area most relevant to their daily experience and will be ready to study a more diverse environment.

SOME MORE EXPERIENCES

You can encourage the children with the following activities:

1 Ask the children to look at the area around them. They should gain a general impression of the whole area and then pay close attention to one particular part of the whole environment. They then come as close as they can to it and concentrate on it with all their attention. They can try to focus their eyes on one part as if they were examining it with a microscope and answer these questions *Does it move? Has it any smell? Is it safe to touch? What colour is it? Does it make any sounds? Can you remember it with your eyes closed? — Look again and check your memory.* They then try looking at it through a rolled up tube of paper; move away a fair distance, eyes nearly closed, and look at it again. The children tell each other as much as they can about their findings.

2 The children can use a magnifying glass to study mosses and lichens, grasses, bark, a drop of water, animal droppings. Give them plenty of time to discuss with others what they find interesting. Guide their thoughts and actions to discovering answers to questions raised by their observations.

3 Tell the children to touch the ground, rocks, tree bark, pebbles, sand and a variety of surfaces with their fingertips, palm of hand, back of hand, knuckles, soft inside arm. If safe, sit on various surfaces stretching out legs, feeling with every part of the body that actually makes contact with a surface. They should concentrate and all the time talk, talk, talk. To themselves, to a friend, to you—the teacher, within a group.

4 Colours can affect moods. Sometimes red, for example, can be overpowering and threatening

yet at other times it makes us warm and happy. Discuss these feelings with the children. Why do some colours refresh, excite, please and delight us, or depress and make us feel miserable? Explore this as far as you can and encourage the children to share their ideas, anecdotes and imaginative thinking with others. Extend their thinking by your own questioning. Feed in appropriate vocabulary and help the children to expand their own. Ask them to show these moods and feelings by pictures, photographs, drawings, movement, song, music, words, phrases, poetry.

5 What influence have light, plants, creatures and minerals on the colour of the environment? What other things influence the colour around us?

6 A further development of grouping could be done with words:
Use other words for blue, red, yellow, green, brown.
Associate emotions with colour.
Describe how these colours make you feel—red, blue, yellow, green, brown, white, orange, purple, pink, black.
Make up categories of your own.

7 Ask the children to describe objects in ways other than talking. They may use drawings, rubbings, subtle washes of colour, textured fabrics, clay or dough, constructions, models, collages. They may want to write. They can compile graphs, charts and sketches from the data collected, which they may prefer to photograph rather than disturb the ecology of the area by removing any specimens.

Make sure you have a wide range of resources for the children to choose from when they come to record their experiences. For too long has writing been regarded as the only valid form of recorded work.

Observe the children closely while they work within the environment. It will give you insights into their skills, attitudes, care of living things, curiosity and ability to work with others.

USING A TAPE RECORDER OR CASSETTE
Encourage the children's development in this area with the following ideas:

☐ Find and bring back sounds that make you feel happy, excited, sad, confident, startled, brave, angry, worried. Compare your sounds and the way they make you feel with other children's sounds. Do the same sounds create the same feelings in everyone?

☐ Record 'playing' sounds and 'working' sounds. See if you can put your sounds together in a rhythmic pattern that you can move to. With the help of other children you may be able to make up a rhythmic chant to go with the sounds.

☐ Take some colour slides of 'working' times and 'playing' times and match them up with your sounds. Make up a story to link the slides together and use the sounds for effect.

☐ Move like some sounds, then move like their opposites. Talk it through with a partner. Other people can be really helpful with ideas. Remember pace and rhythm are important aspects of movement.

☐ There are sounds you like and those you dislike. Record some morning, midday and night sounds. Play them back to friends and see if they can tell what kinds of sound they are and whether they like them or not. Try your different times of day sounds to see if other people can tell when the sounds were recorded.

☐ Cut out silhouette shapes and use them as shadow puppets or use them with an overhead projector. They can look like something real or you can make completely imaginative ones. Join with other children to work out a story and find matching sound effects.

☐ Watch your environment closely; it is full of movement. Find moving things outside and then move like they do. Watch every part of the movement and try to reproduce it exactly. Find sounds like your movements; use your voice or anything from the environment to make the sounds. Compare music that creates the same emotion as the movement. Use percussion instruments or find recorded music that matches.

☐ Let your imagination go wild. Move in a way you've never moved before. Use facial expressions and gestures that you've never used before. Invent some wonderful sounds to match these marvellous movements. Concentrate on your own thinking; don't worry about anyone else.

☐ Go outside and do something you've always wanted to do. Make sure it's safe and you will not hurt yourself or others. It may be a practical thing or just a fun thing. Tell the other children how you felt while doing your thing. Think about what can be done to let more of this kind of activity happen in schools. Think why it might be discouraged. Discuss this with your teacher. Create something that expresses your feelings about doing your thing.

☐ Work with a partner. Take a blindfolded walk touching whatever you're led to and discuss it with your partner. Try to describe how it feels in as many ways as you can.

☐ Wear a blindfold for half an hour. How did you feel? How is the sense of touch affected by feelings? Does it make any difference if you know what the object is?

☐ Using any medium, represent your awareness of texture, shape and mass of the object you have felt but not seen.

☐ Sit in a group of about seven people. Be blindfolded or keep your eyes shut and pass around a variety of objects. Describe each object with words or make up sounds to represent the object.

☐ At night time go outside for a while. At first it will seem to be pitch black but when your eyes adjust to the light you should be able to pick out and identify parts of your environment. Find out more about this change of sight. How does it affect animals?

ALL LIVING THINGS CHANGE

☐ Go outside and prove that this is true. Find some living thing and describe it. Then describe how it is changing, has changed or will change.

☐ Change your own environment. Make a good change or stop a bad change. You may be able to make an immediate difference or your change could take a long time to work. See if you can measure the changes now or if you can predict the size and direction of future change.

☐ Look at your environment closely. Can you find things that will change in an expected or predictable way? Look again and find things changed in ways that could not have been expected. Can you predict changes in yourself?

- Create a set of posters promoting good changes and discouraging bad changes. Can you influence other people's attitudes to their environment by these posters?

- In your environment there will be things that are in the process of increasing. Remember things increase in many ways, not only in numbers. Find something that is decreasing. Now find something that always increases and something that always decreases. Make a group list and keep increasing or decreasing it.

- Write a poem in which the words or lines increase or decrease.

- Make up a riddle or joke about things that change.

- Find something you really dislike in the classroom or outside. See what you can do to change it. You may need others to help you.

- Make a drawing or take a photograph of some of the things you like or dislike. You may cut out pictures in newspapers or magazines. Work with a partner and share your pictures; arrange them in order. Find out if your partner would change the order and, if so, discuss why.

- Find the youngest and oldest things in the school or outside. Make a group mural or a collage of very old things and very young things. Can you describe 'old' and 'young' without actually using those words?

- Our moods change with the weather. Go outside on a windy or rainy day and see how you feel. How do you feel lying on the beach or a grassy slope on a warm day?

- Take ten photographs. You can choose them or select them from a box without looking. Write a story using all the photographs.

- Colours influence the way you feel. Some colours make you feel happy and secure, others depress you. Can you create change to your environment by altering the colours around you? You could make models in cardboard boxes. Why not make your classroom into an environmental change area?

- Look at objects in your environment and compare them with their shadows. Can you explain any differences? Compare them at different times of day.

- Collect some things from your environment and create an art form from them. Make a series where each piece of art shows
  how ugly the environment is
  how beautiful it is
  how the environment makes you feel
  how it has changed through time
  how it has been constructed by people

- Take art materials of your choice outside. Use them on or with some aspect of the environment to bring back some environmental representation (rubbings).

- Collect something outside which would be useful as an art tool. Remember not to damage the ecology when you collect your tool. Create some art; talk, write, compose songs about it.

- Create a mysterious piece of art using the environment for your ideas. Your art could be funny, sad, exciting, frightening or friendly. Try other ideas.

Discussion

When children are on an excursion, try to carry cassette recorders to tape sounds and any relevant discussion. It is advisable to work in small groups, each gathering around areas of specific interest. The reporting back of various groups can be recorded on large sheets of paper and used by the whole grade. This small group organization allows children to focus their attention on particular aspects of investigation rather than trying to relate to the entire area. The teacher can help by supplying simple guidelines for a group to start on and then leaving them to develop the study in their own way. Once the groups are operating independently the teacher can wander from group to group, listening, observing, perhaps contributing. Each individual investigation committee can put their own record together in chapter form and then a book about the excursion is a permanent part of your reading material.

If you are preparing for a camp, use the group organization to discuss a variety of problems beforehand. See what solutions the groups find.

a) A party of children and a teacher are going on a hike. They will be away for three days. What will they need to carry in their packs? How far can they travel in one day? How many rest stops will they need?

b) Study a map of the route; the contours and gradients, signs and symbols, hazards, where north is. Estimate the total distance and the expected rate of covering various distances. Tell officials at the camp your plans for the whole trip. Draw a map of your own camp area using a scale and include a way of crossing the camp. Using a compass, select various prominent features so that you can take position bearings.

c) During the hike someone loses the only compass. You are in dense scrub and there are no prominent symbols on the map to help you. How can you work out the direction to follow? Can you find true north without a compass?

d) On the hike your party has to leave the defined and planned track. Signs must be left for others to follow. What can you use as indicators that will not harm the ecology of the bush? Explain what each indicator means and compile an indicator chart.

e) Two members of the party have become separated from the rest. Report on your walkie-talkie all the details so that a search party can be arranged. Give an accurate description:
Height, age, what they were wearing.
When were they reported missing?
Where were you when they disappeared?
Any ideas of what direction taken?
Type of country?
Any other relevant information?

f) You have to camp for the night. How do you find a suitable site to pitch the tents? Discuss possible danger points; trees, areas subject to flooding, ant nests. Can you use a compass at night?

g) Clear a spot for a campfire. Collect materials; twigs, dry bark, branches, and arrange these so that they will burn freely. The wood is rather damp and the fire smokes making you cough.

What action will you take? When the fire is burning well and there are plenty of glowing coals, wrap your food in aluminium foil and put it in the hot coals. What can you find around the camp site to rake the parcel out of the coals when you think it is cooked? How will you make sure the fire is out before leaving? How will you get rid of the rubbish?

h) The hike is continued to the second camp site. After a night's sleep, the air next morning is very quiet. You look out of the tent and find the whole area looks unfamiliar; it is covered with snow. Will you need to put on more clothes? What games can you play? Your hands get very cold. How will you warm them?

i) Returning to base camp, the snow begins to build up on the soles of your shoes making it difficult to walk. Your feet feel very heavy and walking is an effort. You are dismayed to find you have been walking in circles and you are back at the starting point. What will you do?

j) A member of the party slips down a steep slope and has a badly hurt leg. Unable to walk and in a lot of pain, the patient has to be rescued with ropes you carry and the leg put in a splint. What can you use for a splint and a stretcher?

k) A helicopter is searching for you and is hovering overhead. Can you make a signal on the ground? How do you attract the pilot's attention with something bright? Are you in radio contact?

Preparation for activities outside the classroom

Use the following materials to help children gain some background knowledge of the area they are studying.

Maps
    road
    tourist
    street directories
    aerial photo-maps

Local Information
    tourist brochures
    newspapers
    telephone directories
    National Trust pamphlets
    Historical Society material
    family photographs
    models
    citizens
    by-laws

For Observation
    binoculars
    telescopes
    hand lens
    hand magnifiers
    microscopes
    torches or lanterns
    mirrors

For Collection and Recording
    knife (with sheath)
    wire

corks
transparent plastic sheeting
rubber bands
sieves
shovel
string
funnel
cellulose adhesive tape
clips
pegs
net
masking tape

Containers
    matchboxes
    buckets
    plastic bottles
    egg and milk cartons
    bags
    tins
    large container to carry bits and pieces

Audiovisual Equipment
    video tape recorder
    cassette recorder (with extension lead for microphone)
    slide camera
    polaroid camera
    movie camera
    light meter
    flashlight

Sketching and Writing Materials
clipboard
coloured pens
paper (lined, plain, graph, tracing)
ruler
chinagraph pencil
oil pastels
pencils
paints
rubber
glue
scissors
clay for modelling
plaster and aluminium foil for moulding

Measurement
Distance
ball of string
tape measures
trundle wheel
rulers
callipers
depth gauge

Time
clock
egg timer
watch
tocker timer
stopwatch

Mass
spring balance
scales — kitchen, bathroom, hand

Volume
household bucket
feeding bottle
graduated eye dropper
medicine glass
measuring jugs and cylinders

Temperature
highest and lowest recording thermometer

Miscellaneous
rain gauge
spirit level
pedometer
altimeter
compass
barometer

Interviewing

Children will be asked to go out into the local community to seek information from many sources, and a major activity will be face to face interviewing with a wide range of people. There are many things to consider before letting your class, or part of it, loose on the outside world. Asking other people for their opinions is, for many children, a new and often frightening experience. Children have to realise that they have no automatic right to information and that if people do share their thoughts and feelings with them they do it with trust and the expectation of respect of confidence.

Most people are keen to talk about themselves and the things that are important to them, and if they are approached courteously and responsibly they will respond appropriately. If adults don't wish to answer and evade the interview, the children must accept this without being rude. It is not their place to decide why people do not want to help them nor do they have the skill to make accurate judgments like that.

Here are some specific ways in which a teacher can help and support children who want to conduct interviews.

1 Help the children set out their area of inquiry in some détail. Suggestions can then be made as to whether they can cope with the situation during school hours and the number of children who will be involved.
2 Find out the best people to interview. If the children need specific information they will have to approach a particular person who knows the required facts. If they only want some expressions of attitudes and opinions then they can ask a wider range of people.
3 Make sure that children are able to record information easily (note taking, checklists, cassette and tape recorders, video-pak recording).
4 Give children a note from school indicating the nature of the project, reasons for asking questions, and stating that they have the school's support and approval.
5 If possible, and the interviews are not random, the teacher should contact those to be interviewed before the children visit them.
6 The teacher should arrange for people to come to the school to talk with small groups, or even arrange for visitors to talk to individual children.
7 Give children opportunities to develop their own questions about a project. They will then be more highly motivated to talk to other people as a way of finding 'answers'.
8 Help children understand how valuable the experience of interviewing is to their understanding of the project they are working on. It will mean that they acquire skills in forming questions around a theme; they will gain in confidence from talking to others; they will have a chance to meet and know people they might not normally meet; they will learn that all sorts of people can be a resource, both for information and as a source of new ideas, and they can use the results from asking others as a starting point for further inquiry. Some of the social, sexist and racist attitudes in the local community can be overcome if children have a chance to see local identities occupying alternative roles.

9 The teacher should give children practice in asking questions, within roleplaying situations of small groups talking to a guest speaker. Interview sessions on radio and television should be discussed. Ask the children to nominate other questions that could have been asked. Surely they could do better than the interviewers who ask the overseas jet setter, who has just got off the plane, 'What do you think of Australia?' They could nominate a particular topic and draw up the questions that should be asked and those that should never be asked.

10 The teacher, when discussing the interviewing done by the children, should direct attention to the kinds of questions asked as well as looking at the gathered information.

11 When children become more adept at interviewing as a way of finding information, they will become clearer in their questioning and will be able to focus on specific aspects of their study. This development should be noted by the teacher and can become a part of the evaluation of their growing skill.

12 It is important to make sure the whole situation is relevant to the children's line of inquiry. Don't practise the skill by itself for its own sake. Asking questions is very complicated. It is really difficult to establish clear communication with other people so it is important to take time to decide on the questions which need to be asked and then decide the people to interview for unbiased responses. This skill can be largely acquired in the classroom so that children go out into the community with techniques that will make the activity worthwhile.

13 Arrange for children to work in twos and threes for companionship, relief and security.

14 When children are back in class, collect all the information and interpret the results. See if the children can be led to find significant responses. Discuss positive, negative and neutral reactions and try to analyse the success or failure of the interview/survey technique as a fact finding method.

Before beginning this activity, the first question any teacher should ask is 'Why are the interviews being conducted and what are the children expected to learn from the experience?' Objectives are very important always but, where there is to be contact with other people, they become critical in order to avoid a poor reaction from interviewer and interviewee. Two basic objectives are:

to provide a context in which children can develop social abilities among themselves and, more importantly, between themselves and others;

to simply produce results; facts, statistics or reports.

There are three basic locations for interviews or surveys:

door to door (or person to person)
street interviews; stopping passers-by
group interviews; in schools or meetings

Door to Door
Very applicable for small area studies on most topics and appropriate to children from seven years upwards. It gives the best chance of sustained, thoughtful responses to questions and can be followed up later if necessary. Children feel happy with this technique. One drawback is its heavy reliance on people who are at home during the day—generally mothers with young children or older people who have retired from work. This could provide an imbalance of opinion.

Street Interviews

These will give a larger, broader sample of opinions. There is access to many people without walking for miles. Interviewers should be spaced so that people being interviewed are not stopped several times. A major drawback is that people may not be willing to stop, answer or stay to talk. Children may feel diffident about stopping people.

Group Interviews

This is a quick way of getting answers from a lot of people. It is a good method if you want simple yes/no answers by a show of hands. For example, 'How many children have lunch at school?' Its disadvantages are the need to timetable it very carefully; the tendency for individuals to change their answers when they see what others are doing, and the problem of getting beyond simple yes/no replies.

There are a variety of styles of survey interview, which the children should study in order to choose the one most applicable to a particular situation.

Rigid Questionnaire

This is suitable for all types of interview and is an economic way of conserving time if there is a simple, clear, prepared set of questions. The obvious advantage is that a decision about what is important will get the desired results. The main disadvantage is that there is not much chance to discuss the topic with those being interviewed. This method was used in the *Avalanche* theme when children interviewed the local Shire President, Shire Engineer and Health Officer, who had only limited time and responded well to a very structured questionnaire.

Open-ended Questionnaire

This is a sheet which has basic fixed questions but also some that are more general. It is more applicable to uncertainty about particular points which may need clarification. It gives people a chance to express and develop their opinions. The main advantages are that it is quick, gets answers and, if prepared carefully, is not seen as totally restraining. Its disadvantage is that some people may talk at length.

This method was used in the *Avalanche* theme when children interviewed local residents, who had more time to talk and were more relaxed with the less structured form of interview. They did not feel 'hounded' by the questions and would have rejected the rigid questionnaire method, seeing it as prying and the children as impertinent.

Semi-structured Interview

This is the first of the true interview forms but still retains some of the aspects of a questionnaire. One question is asked and the conversation occasionally steered back to particular issues so that when the interview is completed major points have been covered. It is very useful for getting opinions and attitudes on a whole series of issues, and particularly for learning something about the relationships between varying aspects of people's lives and their personal priorities. The disadvantages are that it takes longer and learning to steer the conversation to cover the prepared list of issues is really quite difficult; children tend to get carried away and forget their lists. Also it is difficult to analyse the results. However, the social interchange is very valuable and enjoyable for the children.

Unstructured Interview

This is totally open-ended and is started by one simple question. For example, 'What do you think of living here?' This should result in a richness of response. It is largely unpredictable and very difficult to extract conclusions but it gives unlimited opportunities for children to hear opinions in depth.

Finding the way

Children need many activities to help them develop the ability to look for and recognise reference objects which will enable them not only to find their way but to describe routes in their immediate school and local environments. When they are confident in their usual surroundings (classroom and school) and have acquired understandings and skills to cope adequately in that environment, then they can go further afield.

USING THE SENSES

☐ Divide the class into groups of five or six and ask each group to select a leader. The leader chooses one child to be blindfolded. This child will walk around the classroom with the spoken guidance of the group members. They must not touch the blindfolded child, but give encouragement with clear, concise verbal directions. These directions will involve the child in safety, discovery and, hopefully, through precision of the language used by the guides, an understanding of the immediate area. Remind the children of the different levels in which the movement is happening. The floor level and feet; the middle level and the groping hands; the upper level where the head must be safe. Sometimes the guides concentrate on movement and safety at their own eye level and forget other danger spots. Stress the need to vary the pace of movement and the size of the stride. When the blindfolded person touches any surface the guides should, without naming the object, discuss its various aspects (smell, sound, touch and, if appropriate, taste). The guides, as caring, concerned people, have a very important task. Give the groups their own areas to work in (the classroom, corridor and other nearby areas). Change the blindfolded person until everyone in the group has a turn. Encourage the children to freely discuss their feelings about being blindfolded, and how they felt about the guiding directions. If a child falls down a step the second before the guides say 'Mind the step', that child may have very strong feelings about the helpers.

☐ Now try the same activity outside. Five or ten metres is far enough and allow the child to have a look at the area before being blindfolded. No tricks, just plenty of care.

☐ In the classroom, place strong smelling objects around for a blindfolded person to identify; oranges, bananas, onions, fish, perfume, methylated spirits in jars, burnt toast, fish and chips. The children can provide you with ideas.

☐ Ask the children to find particular smells in the schoolground environment. Many may be there naturally, but some can be introduced.

☐ Discuss with the children the senses that are most useful in finding the way and list them in order of importance. Discuss whether senses are used differently when in familiar or unfamiliar places.

SIMPLE MAPPING

This activity needs an assortment of card materials, cardboard boxes, glue, matchboxes, newsprint. Before beginning, check whether the children can:

1 Describe the location of objects in relation to themselves.
   a) Ask them to stand facing the back of the room and describe where the door, chalkboard, teacher's table, bookshelves are in relation to themselves (in front, behind, to the left, to the right, above, below).
   b) They should then turn to face a different direction and give the same information.

2 Ask individual children where different objects are in the room relative to the teacher or another child.

   Where is the heater?
   Where are the windows?
   Where are you?

   Form groups of four at the tables and desks where the children are seated. Have each of the four ask the other children questions, testing their ability to give answers showing an understanding of the spatial relationships between two objects.

3 Do the children understand the distinction between right and left? It will help if they have something tied around the right arm. Use mirrors to see what happens when their body image is reflected. What happens to right and left? Use a class discussion picture and point to the right hand side. Ask the children whether it seems to be the right hand side to them. Study the objects in the picture and ask the children to discuss the relationship between different objects using terms 'right' and 'left'. Practise hand shaking; children move around the room shaking hands and greeting one another as they pass. Form a secret society whose members shake hands always with the left hand. If there are any left handed children in the room, discuss the way they use their pencils; how they hold knives and forks; catch a ball in one hand; open doors.

4 Place a table in the centre of the room. Put a child at each corner and ask each one for a description of the position of an object in relation to that child; then, the child in relation to the object. For example, 'the table corner is on the right of me, but I am on the left of the table.'

5 Divide the class into groups of six. Ask each group to think of special spots in the classroom as 'home'. Somewhere they could hide pieces of paper with their names written on. Without telling the others, each child writes a letter inviting a group member to come 'home' for a visit and giving directions for finding 'home'. When the letters are written, the children go in turn to hide their names; the other children turn their backs . No peeping allowed, it spoils the fun. When this is done each child gives an invitation to a neighbour on the right, and off they go following the directions. If the invitee cannot find the required 'home', more directions must be sought. If any child finds a name unrelated to the invitation, it must be returned to its hiding place without comment. The idea is not for a child to be tricked with false clues, but to see how accurate and concise the directions can be. The game can be played initially inside the classroom, and then around the school and its grounds.

6 The children work in pairs at a table or desk, or seated on the floor. One child places a number of objects on the flat surface and the partner is asked where a certain object is relative to the others. The child can describe the position of

SPIDER'S JOURNEY

Start

an object in relation to the edges of the table or desk or a particular spot on the floor, and the partner has to guess which object is meant. Conventional or unconventional measurement units may be used.

7 Ask the children to put some objects on a sheet of paper (newspaper will do). They should be placed randomly and have a variation in size and shape. Draw around the objects in heavy crayon or felt pens before removing them. Have each child draw a map of the route that could take a small creature (a spider, grub, tiny robot from outer space) from one side of the paper to the other, going around the obstacles. As the children draw their routes, ask them to talk to a partner as if they were the creatures taking this great adventure in an unknown land. Ask them to use their imaginations (if the paper shifts, buckles, creases or bends, could it be an earthquake, avalanche, tornado or some action of an alien being?). Stress the creature's very small size.

8 Using the same map, the children write descriptions of a route from one point to another. They exchange descriptions and each child, with different coloured threads of wool, traces the described route.

9 Ask one child to tell the class the route between home and school naming the key features, such as street names, signs, particular buildings that help find the way. Now, take all the children on the described route from school to the home, checking the position markers and at the same time looking for other features that could be used as alternatives.

10 Check the journey with a local district map. Can the children trace the route on the map? See if they can find the street names and special buildings. Help them to read the various features

on the map and see if they can understand the legend.

11 Ask each child to write on a card directions from home to school giving similar details. Place all the cards in a box and select one at random. Read the directions to the children, without revealing the child's name, follow them and find the destination. Do this at appropriate times during the school year.

12 Pose the problem that the children are in a strange part of town and want to get home. Who could they ask for directions or help? Do they know the local tram, train or bus routes? Do they know how to use a telephone to ring their parents? Make a wall chart showing what to do if anyone is lost. Stress the need to avoid panic.

Map/Symbol Game

Cut out all the symbols and their names separately. The children then pick up either a symbol or name and try to find its match. This can be used in many ways; name/symbol cards, matching name and symbol as in the game *Concentration,* or playing *Snap.*

Take A Word Walk

Words leap out at you on buildings and street signs as you walk around a local area. We depend on them for instructions, directions and information. Direct the children's attention to these signs and extend their word awareness from book and chalkboard to the nearby streets and shopping centres. Observe, record, discuss and use the discovered words.

Choose an area to explore and ask the children to make a list of all the words and notices in that area. This will include words on footpaths, shops, walls, posts and any high up on the buildings. With younger children, use a tape recorder to collect the language they use when searching for words and talking about what they say, where they are and what they look like. Older children may prefer to list words, or record them spatially on some form of simplified map. Ask the children for their own ideas on recording the location of words. Do not make the area too large or the task will become tiring. The basic idea is to help the children become more visually sensitive and aware so that they can bring selected detail into focus.

ACTIVITIES

1 List the main words in alphabetical order. Use them as part of a road or shopping dictionary.
2 Find out the exact meaning of selected words.
3 List the words under topics. For example, a *transport* theme could lead to locating special words only found at bus depots, railway stations, tram stops, taxi ranks.
4 List any unusual words or misspelt words.
5 Discuss where the words and notices are located and suggest why they are there.
6 Ask what materials they are made from and attached to.
7 Invent new names for familiar shops or signs.
8 Design the appearance of a new shop.
9 Make a list of old or new trendy words.
10 Find the meanings of abbreviations. For example, *Bros; Pty Ltd; Co.*
11 Draw the various styles of letters.
12 Where are the smallest and largest letters found?
13 Write down the various materials on which words have been written.
14 How many different kinds of lettering style can be found?
15 Write down four words, each of which is written in a different colour.
16 Which words are written on posts? Why?
17 Ask the children to write in their own words the meanings of the following words:
No Loading; Right of Way; Business as Usual; Give Way; Domestic Appliances; TAB; Fashion Lingerie
18 Plan a street with a row of shops. Show the names and notices for each shop.

USING SIGNS IN THE LOCAL ENVIRONMENT

Familiarise the children with signs that they often see. Discuss the value of them in everyday life as indicators that protect and inform people. Younger children can be helped to build up a sight vocabulary of signs by using games such as *Concentration*, *Snap* or *Dominoes*. See how many of the following signs can be read and understood by the children:

Stop	Go
Don't Walk	Walk
Push	Pull
No	Yes
On	Off
In	Out
Hot	Cold
Women	Men
Ladies	Gentlemen
Entrance	Exit
Lost	Found
Go Back	Wrong Way
To Let	For Sale
Lease Now	For Hire
Jobs Vacant	Help Wanted
Situations Vacant	Situations Wanted
Professional Positions	Auctions
Library	Quiet Please
Surgery	Waiting Room
Emergency	Casualty
In-Patients	Out-Patients
Lavatories	Rest Room
Comfort Station	Ladies Lounge
Public Convenience	Toilets
Vacant	Engaged
Danger	Keep Out
Do Not Touch	Beware Of The Dog
Poison	Keep Out Of Reach Of Children
Caution	

No Swimming	No Fishing
Do Not Proceed Beyond This Point	Private Property
Explosives	Trespassers Will Be Prosecuted
Lifesavers Patrol Here	Bathe Between The Flags
No Hawkers	Back In Five Minutes
No Smoking	Highly Inflammable
School Crossing	Pedestrian Crossing
Keep To The Left	Wet Paint
Be Careful	No Parking
Loading Zone	No Standing
Taxi Rank	Bus Stop
Do Not Disturb	Do Not Open
First Class	Second Class
Tourist	Economy
Doctor	Dentist
Keep Off The Grass	Do Not Feed The Animals
No Admittance	Please Enter
Men At Work	Road Under Repair
Deep Water	No Diving
Telephone	Out Of Order
Rubbish Tip	Don't Rubbish Australia
Pay Here	Employment Office
Post Office	Post Here
Telecom	Bank
Now Open	Closed Until Further Notice
Shop To Let	Divided Road Ends
Parking Bay	Shallow Water—Do Not Dive
Beach Closed	
Office Space	Do Not Talk To The Driver
Pay Driver	
Do Not Lean Out Of The Windows	Pull Cord To Stop
No Dogs Allowed	Electric Wires
Ascent	Descent
Bridge Work Ahead	Curves
Winding Road	Narrow Bridge
Flag Man Ahead	Give Way

Cattle Crossing
Crest
Detour
Koalas Cross Here
Half Road Closed
Loose Gravel
Keep Right
No Overtaking On
  Double Lines
Slippery When Wet
No Left Turn
Indicators Show Depth
Stop Look Listen
Railway Crossing
Sharp Curves Ahead
Trucks Entering Highway
State Forest
Reafforestation Area
Accident Ahead
Fragile
Use No Hooks
Open This End

Kangaroos Next 5 km
Crossing
Dip
Subject To Flooding
Soft Edges
New Surface
No Passing On Bridge
No Through Road
Beware of Trucks Turning
Slippery When Icy
No Right Turn
Speed Limit
Slow
School Children
Stock Crossing
Logging Track
National Park
Winding Road
Steep Descent
Handle With Care
This Side Up
Do Not Drop

There are hundreds of signs and it is important that they are part of the school's reading programme. Collect as many as possible and use them on theme charts and on individual cards. Children can sort, match and classify signs. Find graphic signs to discuss and terminate children's understanding.

Most of the signs listed above are warning and negative in nature. Ask the children how they feel about signs constantly saying 'don't do this' and 'don't do that'. Look around the school to see if the signs or notices there are the same. Is it possible to create signs that are more positively worded? Ask the children to invent their own signs for the classroom, school building and school grounds. Let them select signs on individual cards that become starting points for improvised drama situations. Take photographs of signs that are important to the children. As you walk around the local area with the children help them 'read' their environment. They can relate what they see to what they know and understand about their own locality, be it garden gnomes, grapevines or graffiti. Take them to the city where they can see a completely different type of building with forecourts, huge rock arrangements, sculpture and intricate paving designs. Let them compare the modern with the old and help them become more visually sensitive. Encourage them to make maps of the areas they visit showing things that are important to them so that they will have the opportunity to show what they know about the space in which they move.

Not everything that tells us something about our environment is indicated by signs. There are many images and symbols for children to read. As you take the children around an area, ask how they identify the following:

Chemist
Newsagent
Real Estate Agent
Antique Shop
McDonald's
Pizza Hut
Kentucky Fried Chicken
Bank

Car Sales Yard
Petrol Station
Hotel
Chinese Restaurant
Opportunity Shop
Trash and Treasure
Fish Shop
Town Hall

Take the children to the local butcher shop (Macelleria) and point out the overall images of the shop; even without the meat or if they are too young to read. There will be a particular type of painting on the windows (lots of red and white), pink fluorescent lighting, blue and white striped awnings, plastic grass dividers, bunches of parsley.

Draw attention to the water sliding down the fish shop window, the multi-coloured flags fluttering over the used car yards, the logos for banks and insurance companies. Help the children become aware of the language (graphic, written and imaged) surrounding them and make it basic to your language programme.

If children feel proud of their knowledge of local areas and are able to find their way around fairly independently, you can expect them to investigate a wider area with much more sensitivity and confidence. They will be able to go on to more sophisticated mapping and will be ready for compass work and orienteering techniques because of these initial experiences.

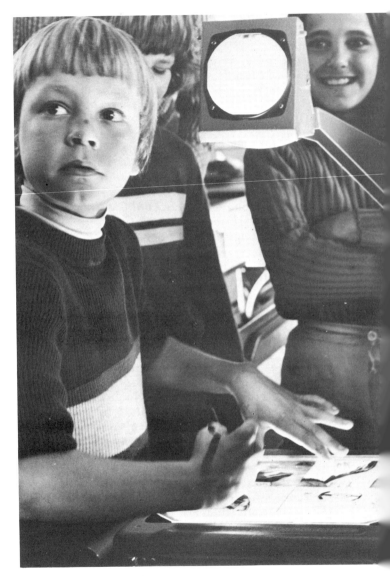

Using the overhead projector for creative storytelling and writing

Overhead projectors are often overlooked as a useful aid in classrooms. Children can be trained in the use of the overhead projector and will find it a wonderful way of presenting their material. The following activities can be used as starting points:

1 Draw maps on a transparency using water based colour pens. Maps can be used for following directions and self-explanatory dictionary skills and meanings. Magi-maps can be similarly treated.
2 Detailed science diagrams can be similarly represented. One child can explain the details to a group of children. For example, how a fish breathes; how echo waves assist in locating fishing grounds.
3 In reading, comprehension puzzles can be set to discover the correct answer in interpretative comprehension exercises. For example, there are four alternatives, either written or illustrated, and children select the correct solution.
4 Telegrams, cables, notices, invitations, letters can be prepared on transparencies. When projected on a screen, these can be viewed by all children and comments and modifications made.
5 The equipment can be used for a television screen presentation with a range of responsibilities for a number of children (illustrator, reader, commentator). Other children become sound effects personnel utilizing records for background music, or percussion instruments and improvised material can be used. Colour can be used on transparencies or coloured transparencies can be utilized. Simple reflectors can be made from coloured cellophane and used on the overhead projector reflector.
6 A story can be told by one child and, as the story is being related, another child draws on the transparency. As the story continues, the transparency is rolled to allow the illustrator to draw the next sequence. This method is repeated until the story is completed, thus presenting the story and pictures in logical sequence.
7 Cartooning is another way to tell a story in logical sequence. Such cartooning should show feelings or emotions by expressions, or in the case of animals by the position of eyes, ears, tail. The movement action should provide added atmosphere and sound effects could also be used.
8 Film making techniques, far distance, middle distance, close-up, can be discussed.

CREATIVE STORY TELLING WITH MUSIC

Here are three ways to utilize material for this activity:
  with transparencies
  with paper cut-out shadow puppets
  a combination of transparencies and puppets

With Transparencies

Before preparing a transparency, children must think of the characters and scene requirements for their story. Help them develop this activity by providing an outline, or the children can develop their own story. The following example will provide ideas for further development.

The Saga of Creepy Grim
Creepy Grim, the cat burglar, robs a factory and escapes across the courtyard, through the park, down an alleyway, across a busy intersection and is apprehended by police.

The children are divided into three groups. Using three large sheets of white paper, group 1 children make three large drawings; one each of the factory, courtyard and park.

Encourage discussion of the requirements for each illustration.

Factory
How many floors in the factory?
On which floor did the robbery take place?
What time of day was it?
Are there downpipes, ladders or a fire escape?
What does Creepy Grim look like
What equipment would Creepy Grim carry?

Courtyard
Is it illuminated or in darkness?
What are the possible obstacles?
How would Creepy Grim climb a brick wall?
What kind of grappling gear would be needed?
Is there a night watchman or security guard
 service?

Park
How big is the park?
Where are the paths, major trees, light fixtures?
Is the park fenced all around?
Are there locked gates?

On each page three words are written:
   Sound   Movement   Feeling
For the factory drawing, children compile all the words for sound associated with that section of the story; similarly for movement and feeling. Such words could be single words, phrases, alliteration.

How would Creepy Grim feel when the dynamite exploded the safe and cracked the windows?
Children express different points of view.

Available percussion material can be used to create sounds for movement and feeling in that section of the story. A double bongo drum might give a heart beat effect for Creepy Grim.

A similar procedure is adopted for the courtyard and park.

Group 1 is now ready to tell the story.

A cardboard cut out of Creepy Grim is mounted on a stick and the story teller uses this when telling the story so that other children can follow the burglar's progress. The children allotted sound effects tasks make the appropriate sounds as the story progresses. When the story teller comes to the end of the park section, the story must be left open ended for the story teller in group 2 to continue. The cut-out figure is handed over to this story teller who continues to maintain the flow of the story.

Group 2 also has three large sheets of paper joined together depicting the alleyway. The children discuss what sounds could be in the alleyway (sounds coming from different houses, rubbish bins, bottles, cats, dogs. There might be a party in one house.) Similar procedures with movement and feeling are followed and the compiled story continues.

The large sheets of paper for group 3 depict well illuminated busy intersections, theatre crowds, restaurants, crowded streets, traffic, policemen. Sounds, movement and feeling are discussed as before and the group 3 story teller concludes the story.

From this practice exercise the children can prepare transparencies using sound effects and story telling on the overhead projector. Coloured cellophane reflectors can give added atmosphere. There would be one storyteller, two children interchanging transparencies, one or two using coloured reflectors, and the remaining children in the group would be the sound effects personnel.

Cardboard Cut-Outs (Shadow Puppets)

The children decide on scenes, characters, animals, objects. A tropical scene would include palm trees, clouds, moon with characters of a traveller and two natives. The animal could be a monkey and the object a coconut.

Each cut-out can be easily moved by attaching florist wire with masking tape. Children can experiment with coloured cellophane for a hot humid night or a moonlight night, and a suitable record can be used to provide a soft musical background. Percussion instruments or improvised materials can be used for effects. Cassette recorders can be used in conjunction with the overhead projector material.

Children should be encouraged to use their own initiative for such creative story telling and a record of the story can be kept for later use. This should include the transparencies, shadow puppets, tapes and the written story.

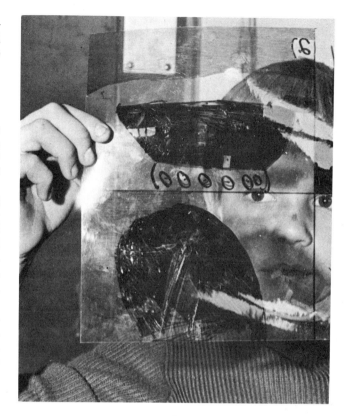

Other Ideas

    Dragon (type of dragon, where it lives)
    Cars
    Butterflies
    Pop singer and guitar
    Three Blind Mice in a polluted city

Combining Transparencies And Shadow Puppets

Puppets can be superimposed on a transparency.

Problem solving

Schools are designed by architects for children and teachers and classrooms are the working space. The approaches today to discovery learning often have to be attempted in buildings and with furniture that was designed for very different teaching methods. Traditional schools were planned on the basis of the whole class unit. It was understood that children would be deskbound most of the time and that books and equipment would be handed out to them by the teacher or monitors. The work was highly teacher directed and the talk was mainly teacher to child. This arrangement does not suit our present thinking, so let us look critically at the classroom or learning area and see if the space can be put to better use.

The school makes a logical base or starting point because it is the one common element in the children's environment. They may all have homes and families but these are different and distinctive for each child. Usually children are most interested in trying to find answers to problems that they have posed themselves. There are problems enough in any school to justify the following investigation.

Present the problem to the children and discuss the following issues:

Does the present arrangement allow a variety of areas for different activities?
Does the furniture need to be designed or re-designed?
Is there too much noise in the room?
Does the room get too hot?
Is the lighting adequate?
What do you think of the colours in the room?

A general discussion of these issues should provide a wide range of opinion and argument. Record major features of the discussion and direct the children to further investigation:

How much time do you spend in the classroom?
How much of your waking time is this?
What sort of activities do you actually do in your classroom?
On what activity do you spend the most time?
What sort of area does the major activity need?
Does your present area suit that need?
What do you like about your classroom?
What do you dislike about your classroom?

There are many ways to encourage investigation of the immediate environment. Challenge the children to initiate actions that will result in some good change. They will learn many mathematical, science, social science and language arts skills quickly in the context of their investigation into real problems. The interdisciplinary nature of real and practical problem solving offers a tremendous opportunity to widen and enrich every area of learning.

Ask the children to look at particular aspects of school or community life. Make sure they feel their efforts are useful and will lead to some improvement in the situation under investigation. If they can expect their findings to be implemented in the short or long term, they will have an increased commitment to finding solutions for the problems.

We are going to look at the following situations: the classroom; the play area; traffic around the school; an emergency in the local area.

THE CLASSROOM

Challenge the class by focussing on a central issue. The children will need to initiate action to respond to this challenge. The nature of the activities will encourage more child-to-child interaction and more small group work as the children collaborate in their efforts. It is the teacher's responsibility to assist their acquisition of necessary skills for problem solving, which include: defining the problem; observing the situation; collecting relevant data; representing and analysing data; making some judgment on evidence gathered; forming and trialling possible solutions; deciding on final action to be taken.

This study can be done by individuals or small groups of children and recorded in different ways: photographs, sketches, written or verbal reports, tape recordings, overhead projector transparencies, graphs, collections.

Ask the children to find out if other children in their own class and in other classes in the school have similar or different opinions to those they have presented.

They should now consider the following questions in regard to the design of the working area:

What learning activities take place in this area?

How many children are involved in the various activities?

What working space will be needed (table top, work bench, horizontal or vertical space)?

What equipment will be needed for each activity?

How will equipment and materials be stored?

Where will the children put their personal possessions?

What movement will there be around the room?

Where will the noisy activities be located?

How can quiet areas be created?

What sort of floor surfaces are needed in the various areas?

By now the children should have fairly well covered the first five aspects of problem solving. They have defined, observed, collected, represented and analysed. They are up to making some judgment on the gathered evidence.

How could *you* make the classroom a better place to work in?

What kind of changes would you like to make?

Set up study groups so that the children can focus on particular aspects. For example, new seating arrangements; decoration; noise level survey; design of new equipment.

The groups will need to solicit opinions from other children and may draw up questionnaires to test opinions. They will have to find possible solutions to the problems and, in consultation with the Principal, School Council, parents and teachers, try to implement the changes that are mutually decided upon as a result of their investigations and recommendations.

THE PLAY AREA

A great deal of learning takes place outside the school. Many important learning experiences can take place on the school site if the school environment is planned with this understanding. The outside of the school should be an extension of the inside. Provision for the following should be made:

physical activity
imaginative activity
social learning
environmental study
mathematics and science
exploring materials
extensions of classroom activity

Ask the children to look at the school play areas, inside and outside, to see if they could be improved. They can draw a plan of the site indicating the school buildings, hard surface areas and paths, games areas and their surfaces, the area available for free play.

Where is the adventure playground situated? Can a list be made of the activities and games played in these areas? Indicate on the plan the storage areas for playground and sports equipment. Show the shelter sheds and say whether they are used for shelter or as storage rooms for equipment. Indicate the direction of the prevailing wind and mark in the seats, benches, sandpits, barbecues, shrubs and trees. Show the areas that are sunny and those in shadow most of the time. If some areas are allotted on age or sexual differences, indicate that on the plan. Do dangerous limbs on trees or old stumps make hazards and put play areas out of bounds? Mark in the bicycle racks and indicate whether they are under cover. Show areas that are not available for playing (teachers' car parking space, windows, shrubbery, toilets, incinerator or waste disposal dumper). What provision is made for the disposal of rubbish around the school? Show where the bins are usually placed. Are there enough of them and are they in the best place for children's use? Are there factories or mills nearby? Are they a likely cause of pollution? Mark heavy traffic nearby that interferes with the working conditions of the school. Indicate the drinking troughs and taps. Is the water adequate for the number of children? If there are water tanks when were these last cleaned? Have filters been placed in the tanks to keep the water clean? If some areas suffer from after school or weekend vandalism indicate these also. There are hundreds of things to find out about in an ordinary school ground. Ask the children how they see their playing areas and table all the information given. Discuss the following issues:

Is there adequate space for games?
Is there enough equipment?
If not, what sort of equipment is needed?
Is there proper use of equipment?
Is there adequate storage and distribution of equipment?
Do some children monopolize space and equipment?
What equipment gets most use and why?
What equipment gets least use and why?
Is there unfair restriction on the use of areas or equipment simply on sexist or age criteria? (Examples would be little children not allowed on certain areas and girls not allowed on the football oval, usually prime areas.)
Are there enough attractive seating areas?
Are there different surfaces and levels?
Is the playground surface in good condition?
Is any equipment dangerous (monkey bars too high)?
Can the school grounds be beautified by tree planting?
Are there any areas that would attract birds to the school?
Are there ways to conserve water and prevent wastage?
Are any of the logs or old timber lying around harbouring dangerous insects or snakes?
Are some areas of the school ground waste space?
If so, how could they be fully utilised?

Ask the children to check the condition of the equipment and the accident register over the last five years to see if any have been caused by faulty equipment or badly surfaced areas; check which grades use particular equipment or areas.

Questions to stimulate further investigation:
What do you like to do on the playgrounds?
What are some of the things you do not like about the playgrounds?
Where do you like to play inside the school?
What do you do there?
How could you improve your play areas?
What sort of changes would you like to make?
What new equipment would you like to have?
Could you build any new equipment?
Could your parents build any new equipment?
Is it easy to be hurt on equipment? List dangers.
How often should equipment be changed?
Can you swap equipment with another school?

Take the children to visit local playgrounds and park areas to gather ideas. Take photographs of equipment or areas that impress you.

Check catalogues to find out costs of equipment if you intend to make changes. Contact Education Department officers in Educational Design and Physical Education sections for assistance. Visit the school nurseries for advice on tree and shrub planting.

When the children have received the advice they require, help them to prepare itemised lists of equipment needed with the priorities indicated. They should be able to show the following:
   the equipment needed
   who will look after it (class, group, individual or teacher)
   how much work it will take
   how much it will cost
   where it can be obtained

With all this data collected they can present recommendations to the Principal and School Council, who will decide:
   whether the equipment can be afforded out of present funds
   if it can be purchased over a period of time
   whether equipment can be improvised with the help of parents
   if fund raising should be initiated for this specific purpose

TRAFFIC AROUND THE SCHOOL

The area surrounding the school provides excellent study opportunities. Many schools take children miles away for excursions and neglect the immediate surroundings. A study of the local area is desirable before venturing further afield. The problem posed here is an investigation of the traffic flow and how it affects the children. Use information from local street maps and draw a plan of nearby streets, major buildings, shops, houses and major traffic intersections. Drawn on large sheets of paper and pinned on the wall at child level, the children can fill in the details that are meaningful to them. See if each child can have a street directory map of the area. Discuss the following:

   major roads and streets
   pedestrian crossings
   school crossings
      Do the children understand the use of the red flags?
      Are parked cars causing congestion and danger?
      Do motorists observe the crossing rules?
      Do the children observe the crossing rules?
   traffic controls
      by lights
      by police officers
   ways to reach the school by public transport
   bicycle safety
   school bus system
      What are the safety considerations for children getting off buses?

Draw a map showing the routes and distances travelled by individual children each day

Give a timetable for daily travel

Show major traffic factors (crossroads, bridges, railway crossings, viaducts)

Indicate bus shelters; visibility or obstructions at pick-up points

made roads; roads under construction; roads subject to flooding; hazards (animals crossing, stock routes, timber truck entry to highway, road surface subject to ice or frost, winding roads, bridge crossings)

finding the way to school

how each child gets to school

overpasses and underpasses

road signs

Take children to areas with these problems:
Narrow streets clogged by parked cars
Trams occupying the middle of the road
Buses pulling in and out of traffic
Heavy industrial traffic
Trucks and vans unloading goods
Divided highway with plantation areas to cross
Busy shopping centre
Railway crossings
   with gates
   with barriers
   with flashing lights
   without flashing light signals

Assist them to define the problems by close observation of the various areas. They must collect information and suggest alternatives if they consider the areas unsatisfactory. Ask them to discuss the similarities and differences they have noticed in the traffic flow in the places they have seen. Some of these alternatives could evolve:

Rerouting of traffic by means of one way streets
Imposing parking restrictions
Construction of overpasses or underpasses
Pedestrian crossings
Speed restrictions
Traffic lights
Police control
Parking officers
Goods vans required to make early or late deliveries

Investigations could include counts of cars going in different directions and making different turns, measurements of car speeds, volume and density of cars in the problem sections at different times of the day.

Remember to use study groups so that a small number of children can concentrate on a specific issue.

Children could make scale models of proposed changes and use them to simulate traffic flow (under the proposed changes) using the information they have gathered. Make sure they are directed to photographs, plans and sketches of traffic features like flyovers, clover leaf constructions, tunnels.

Provide them with resource material and encourage them to find information themselves. Build up a collection and what they cannot find they can then construct themselves.

Contact the local police and arrange for them to talk to the children about safety rules for pedestrians, bicyclists, motor cyclists, cars, trucks, public transport; bad accident spots in the district; local hazards and how they could be improved; obedience of drivers to traffic regulations; police opinion of the effectiveness of police control of traffic compared to traffic lights; the use of police horses in traffic control; legal aspects of pedestrian safety; which local pedestrian crossing has the best record and why; which local pedestrian crossing has the worst record and why; what they do when they see a motorist break the law (go through against a red light); comparison of problems encountered by motorists, bicyclists, pedestrians; children's behaviour as a factor in road safety; the time of day that traffic is heaviest/lightest, fastest/slowest; the most dangerous weather conditions; the pedestrian age group involved in most accidents and why; the motorist age group involved in most accidents and why; the most likely vehicle to be involved in a serious accident.

Provide time for the children to make a report of their findings to the police and encourage them to make recommendations. Record this session so that the children can play it back at later times to check the particular aspect of information referring to their own group's study area.

Take the children around the immediate area again and tackle these issues:

Road Signs
Examine their placement and condition. Can smaller children see them? Can they read and understand them? Does the use of symbols make signs easier to understand? Make a chart of the various road signs. Photograph any that are not helpful for children and say what is wrong with them.

Roads And Footpaths
Look at the condition of the roads and footpaths in the immediate vicinity of the school. Ask children to check the condition of their own streets. Why are some better than others? Document possible hazards and take photographs to be presented to the local council or road authority. Take photographs of very good roads or streets so that a comparison can be made.

Parental Opinion
The children ask their parents about streets that are troublesome to drive through. List the problems and suggested improvements.

Community Opinion
Ask the local home owners and shopkeepers for their ideas; mothers with prams, adults with shopping jeeps if they find the footpaths too steep; elderly people if they find the roads and footpaths dangerous. Find out if there has been any thought given to the problems of handicapped people in the area.

Differences In Roads
Observe and record the differences between one way streets and two way streets. Find the differences between roads and motorways; local streets and inner city streets. List these differences.

The children may think of many other things they would like to study. The information now gathered should enable them to make some judgments about traffic around the school and they should be in a position to present certain recommendations to the local authorities.

A case study: Landslide

AN EMERGENCY IN THE LOCAL AREA

After heavy rain the Melbourne to Sydney highway was blocked by flooding at Seymour. Civil authorities and the army personnel at Puckapunyal army camp were called in to evacuate and rescue people in the flooded sections of the town and nearby farms. At the same time at Trawool, a few miles from Seymour on the Seymour-Yea road, there was an enormous landslide which blocked the highway. Teachers at the Seymour East school decided to examine the situation and see if they could safely take a group of children out to the landslide. Permission was granted and the teachers began to motivate the children towards the development of a theme, *Landslide.* Experience gained by pupils, of flooding in the area and the personnel involved, was incorporated for the purpose of the *Landslide* study.

This unit is a record of how the theme was developed. It records more than actually happened as, apart from the children's findings, the teacher recorded other activities that could have been followed. Other children and teachers may have developed the theme very differently and obviously there are many shortcomings in the theme development. However, it did happen along these lines and we hope it may be a useful model.

Planning timetable

1 Teachers visited the landslide area.
2 They checked the suitability of the site for student activity and study.
3 Teachers contacted the appropriate authorities for permission to visit and checked whether the children would be safe from hazards; also that they could have a good look around without interfering with the clearing operation.
4 Newspaper reports were collected. Children reported on radio and television broadcasts.
5 Suitable transport was arranged with bus company and costs estimated.
6 Teachers sent to parents all necessary details about the excursion together with indemnity forms.
7 Librarians at the school and municipal libraries were asked to find relevant literature. The children also checked their own resources.

Pre-excursion activities in the classroom

Displays; assignments; discussions; study of film and filmstrip catalogues for suitable material; book research; maps, mapping; list of needed resources; children's flow charts; talk on safety precautions; science activities with water flow on earth; study of sound effects, percussion and records.

Day before the excursion

There was a check on study materials to be taken. Children were advised as to suitable clothing and footwear. All the returned indemnity forms were checked and money collected for the bus.

Follow up activities

Flow charts were revised. New possibilities and new interests had been stimulated because of the direct experience. Interest groups were formed and children began to plan their areas of study.

Pre-visit

In the pre-visit discussion, the focus was on the disruption of services because of the blocking of the highway. The teacher posed the problem:

What effect would such a disruption have on the lives of the people in that community?

From class and group discussions the following points were noted in this very simple flow chart:

The children decided they would have to gather information mainly by their own observation with a possibility that local residents might help answer some questions. They were quite aware that they could not approach the workers. Cameras, cassette recorders, measuring tapes, magnifying glasses, field glasses, maps, plastic bags and jars for specimen collection were organised.

The teacher stressed the need for safety precautions when the children arrived at the site. Group leaders were chosen and the groups drew up their own safety rules. These were then reported back to the whole class for advice or criticism. The adult assistance, other teachers and volunteer parents, was organised.

Excursion

The buses stopped in the safety area and the group proceeded on foot. Children looked for signs and found *detour, hazard, washout.* There were also flashing amber warning lights. The power and force of the water was indicated by broken concrete culvert pipes, pieces of fence and debris in the washout, boulders, dead animals, silt. Children made notes, collected samples and took photographs. They studied the disruption (one part of the road was just a gaping hole), and saw how and where the traffic had been diverted.

They looked at the warning devices and the road surface of the diversion. Some looked for imprints of vehicles, heavy machinery, animals and people. The nearest buildings were noted. The children determined the highest water level indicated and could see that it was receding. They photographed workers using power saws on the fallen trees and also the SEC workers dealing with fallen power lines. The children entered the paddocks and, at a safe distance, were able to see the steepness of the slope; material that had shifted and where it was deposited (they were impressed by the size of the boulders). Discussion was about the loss to the farmers of valuable grazing land and the effect this would have on stock; loss of stock; loss of production. They were concerned about the need to provide the remaining stock with fodder and water and also the need for the farmers to replace damaged farm machinery. They were aware that vegetation and pastures would have to be reclaimed and became very concerned about compensation as it was not the farmers' fault. The teachers reassured them that there was primary production insurance and farmers could apply for government assistance through their local Member of Parliament. There were crickets in the earth and one group became very interested in the possible damage to animal life in the soil and local area. Some became fascinated by the strewn rocks and boulders and were measuring and chipping off samples for later study.

Communication became the next centre of interest, and the following points were discussed:

1 Mail, phone, papers would be disrupted.
2 The role the media plays in warning people.
3 Maps should be displayed showing diversion.
4 Helicopters could be used in surveying area.
5 Ways of reporting the disaster—radio, television, newspapers.

6 Workers would need ways of communicating. Children suggested megaphones, walkie-talkies, signs and signals.

7 Emergency groups would be required. This led to the following discussion on health:

Animals — dead animals, blowflies, smell, decay, life cycles, scavengers, removal of dead stock in case of disease.

People — need for clean water supplies; children collected samples of pond, stream and tank water to study with microscopes; food supplies have to be maintained to all people affected by the disaster.

Injuries — cuts, scratches, fractured limbs or head injuries; need for immediate first aid; fear of infection.

Evacuation — injured people have to be kept warm and given rest; ambulances and stretchers are needed.

Other things mentioned were community effort, sightseers, looting. Some of the local farmers were prepared to be interviewed and were asked these sorts of questions:

Where were you when it happened?
What were you doing when it happened?
Did you have any warning?
What do you think about it?
How do you feel when you see the damage?
How did you communicate with other people?
Did you have to leave your home?
Where did you go?
How long do you think it will take to clear up?

The children were in groups of five for their interviews and used cassette recorders. The Local Mayor invited the groups to attend a council meeting in the new council chambers.

Back in the classroom, each group gave its report and re-played tapes of interviews. The teacher and the children noted down facts they considered interesting or important. A revised and more detailed class flow chart was constructed and groups formed for their interests. However, each group realized that grouping would be flexible as all children would be interacting and sharing similar interests and activities at different times.

REVISED FLOW CHART

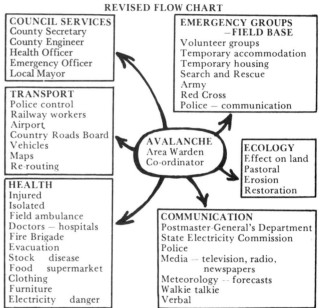

The children decided to approach the local municipal council and request interviews to further their research activities. Permission was received from the County Secretary, County Engineer, Health Inspector, Local Mayor, Social Welfare Officer and Emergency Officer for small groups to visit the municipal offices. The children formulated the types of questions they would like to ask prior to the visits.

County Secretary

What is the council's role in times of local disaster?

Is there a co-ordinator of services? If so, what is his/her role?

How does the County Secretary keep communication continuing between all bodies?

What are the duties of the secretarial staff?

How does the national government co-operate with local government in such an emergency?

If an emergency council meeting has to be held, what papers do you prepare for such meetings?

County Engineer

What is your role when roads and bridges are damaged?

What types of materials are required?

What emergency equipment is used for rapid repair of bridges?

Does the Country Roads Board assist in this work and how?

Would the army provide Bailey bridges and heavy equipment?

What alternative routes are recommended for heavy traffic?

What are the roles of the specialist staff in the engineer's branch of the County?

Health Officer

What is the Health Officer's role in relation to a disaster?
  a) injured people
  b) emergency services
  c) emergency housing
  d) food provision and handling
  e) disposal of rubbish
  f) disposal of dead stock
  g) co-ordination of volunteer groups

What other health hazards could be anticipated?

Would there be any need for immunization?

Emergency Officer

What is the role of such a person?

Do any other organisations assist?

What is their role?

How do local welfare organisations assist?

How are emergency workers housed?

What halls are utilized and how are they used?

What relief (food, clothing, bedding) is organised for emergency helpers?

How is this financed?

Who co-ordinates search and rescue, hospital, ambulance, doctors, police teams?

Local Mayor

What is the Local Mayor's role during a disaster?

What public relations work is necessary?

How does he/she keep in touch with what is happening?

General concern was expressed for loss of stock, damage to homes, fences, equipment, inconvenience caused, restoration; also the need for national government relief assistance.

Each group then looked at how they would organise themselves.

1 Research

Possible activities; discussions and what would be discussed; posing problems; interviews; visits and visitors; books; magazines; newspapers; maps; films.

2 Resources

Cassette recorders; cameras; overhead projectors; science equipment; books (research); films; slides; newspapers; maps.

3 Recording and application

Re-enacting; cassette and camera; note taking; booklets; charts; stories — factual, imaginative; vocabulary — spontaneous, specialised; art and craft; experiments; conclusions.

After preparation of a plan, and allocation of duties and responsibilities to members of the group, activities could be initiated. However, there would be the necessity for groups to revisit the site for more detailed observation and study.

Communication
The children conducted interviews with local residents.

Farmers

Where were they at the time of the disaster; immediate thoughts and feelings; receive prior warnings or not? If out in the fields, were they in danger and how did they avoid injury; first thoughts and reactions; difficulties experienced in reaching home or maintaining contact with families; measures taken to save stock and equipment?

Farmer's Wife

What warning did she receive? How she felt, terrified; anxious about her husband somewhere in the fields? What she felt when unable to contact anyone by telephone; when special news bulletins were heard on the radio; when the area was blacked out; when she heard the rumbling of the landslide; concern for the rest of the family?

Hotel Proprietor or Storekeepers

The effect on trade and customers; how they assisted; how messages were conveyed to other people in the community; community involvement?

Police Officers

Number of people in the area; survey of houses?

How many people to be evacuated; to remain; isolated; injured; missing; dead; loss of stock? Supplies available and those needed; how would these supplies and assistance get to the area; ability to follow directions from a map?

PMG Workers

Statement of telephone services and emergency services available; range of these emergency services and telephones; means of maintaining communications with disaster organisers and media?

SEC Workers

Restoration of power; removal of limbs and trees; dangers of electrocution; fires?

Discovery
Observing damage that has disrupted communications; emergency restoration; the work of police; road maintenance teams; re-directing traffic; evacuation of people; stock; weather; direction of rain; cloud cover; shaded areas; sightseers; signs; helicopters; two-way communication; field telephones.

Follow up activities
The groups, on return to the classroom, decided they would publish a newspaper in relation to the landslide and write news bulletins for television and radio. This required members to be assigned to special duties as news reporters, interview reporters, camera operators, illustrators, editorial staff, classified advertisements section. This leads to presentation of the newspaper, television (evening news and interviews), radio bulletins. Children had roving capacities to interview pupils in other groups and collate their material.

Photographs taken at the scene of the disaster were developed and recorded information on cassettes was transcribed to paper and mounted beside the photographs. This provided a language experience approach arranged in logical sequence. Other photographs were used for dictionary skills as words mounted beside pictures became labels to understand words associated with objects in the photographs.

Children re-enacted the roles of interviewer and people initially interviewed at the scene. Here children had to 'feel' their roles and emotions had to be identified. From interaction within the groups, ideas for further interviews arose. For example, Red Cross worker, government representatives, injured person.

Experiments were conducted with improvised percussion for sound effects in relation to the landslide (like the roaring of a train), or people and animals associated with 'after the event' scenes. These were to be used in television presentation of news. Classified advertisements ranged from flood warnings (closed roads, detours) in the public notices to lost and found notices (stock, people); for sale (boat, horse, sheep, cattle, farm, house); remedies (crutches, wheelchairs, ointments, bandages); equipment (bulldozers, tractors, pulleys).

Situations were set up for messages to be conveyed by a variety of means—walking, horse, bicycle, vehicle (car, truck, motorcycle), boat, railway trolley, morse code, two-way radio (ground search-rescue; police, rural fire brigade, SEC), telephone, radio and television, air spotter in control tower.

Reports

The children discussed the municipal council meeting and important information that arose. They also discussed holding a council meeting of their own.

How many councillors and whom would they represent? What important matters would they be likely to raise at the meeting? Council officers and what reports would they make? Would the press be represented? How many people would be permitted in the gallery?

A President was elected and meeting procedures discussed. How is a motion put? How many times could a speaker speak on a motion? Voting – who has the casting vote?

Then pupils held their own council meeting. Representatives were chosen to inverview a State government officer seeking relief assistance and **compensation for farmers. 'The County Secretary to write to the Premier stating the extent of damage and hardship'.**

The disaster newspaper was compiled with every child sharing and contributing.

For the news session on television the overhead projector was used as a television screen for presentation with the news reader (maps plus commentary, illustrations plus 'on the spot' reporter) with the illustration being shown as the item of news is commented on by the reporter. Shadow puppets with sound effects and colour cellophane for mood were used for other dramatic news presentations. Weather reports with maps on transparencies and a weather reader. This presentation was followed by a current affairs session where students from other groups conducted their own discussions on ecology, erosion, reclamation, government involvement and compensation, insurance.

Weather charts and forecasts

A study of weather maps in daily papers to understand the construction of a weather map and the various terms used (cold front, warm front, high and low pressure, winds, force of winds, rainfall).

Rainfall was recorded on a daily basis from the school's rain gauge. Cloud cover was observed for density, height, type of clouds in relation to amount of rain. Condensation and precipitation experiments were performed, (any science book has examples of these). A simple anemometer was made to measure the speed of wind.

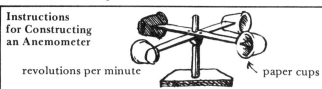

Instructions for Constructing an Anemometer

revolutions per minute ← paper cups

Make a wooden base with a round piece of dowel for an upright. Cross-arms of equal length are made from flat pieces of lightweight wood joined in the centre at right angles. At this central point a hole is drilled to allow the arms to rotate on the dowel. To prevent the arms from slipping down, attach plasticine or play dough. Paper drinking cups are attached at the end of each cross-arm. Colour one cup to use as an indicator for counting the number of revolutions as the cup passes over a predetermined mark.

A weather vane showed the direction of the wind. These results were then compared with weathering on trees, fences, buildings (prevailing winds). Weather forecasts were compiled. Background from newspapers, television and locals who have predicted weather over a number of years. Some claimed that the stars and moon indicate future weather patterns. Children looked on the latter as superstition but were set a task to see if there was any truth in such forecasts. Rainfall figures and river heights were then given. Nearby, at a bridge over the river, was a river height marker gauge which could be used for measuring rises and falls and graphs constructed. Daily and monthly rainfall figures were recorded in the same manner. The 'wet season' could be identified and the possibility of floods and landslides. Months for precautionary measures were noted.

Mapping

In conjunction with a 'transport' group various types of maps were studied including road, strip, aerial photo, council zone and army survey maps.

To enable the children to read maps much preliminary reading of simple maps was required. These included a plan of the school and schoolgrounds, section of town with houses and shops, a simple map of towns, roads and railways. Studying these simple maps developed skills relating to:

a) position of a house or town in relation to another building or town
b) direction from A to B
c) shortest way to travel
d) scale
e) signs and symbols

Further skills to be developed with strip maps to survey maps: kilometre posts (distance to bridge, town); towns not on highway; population of towns; alternative routes; distance as the crow flies; contours on mountains. Making a relief map of area affected showing position of road, railway, bridges, streams, houses, steepness of mountain, valley.

Use a model to explain phenomena of landslide, disruption, search and rescue, model transport, relief workers, emergency housing. Compare actual site of mishap with map. Where would warning signs be placed? What type of transport would be permitted in the area?

An area is impassable. Traffic has to be diverted and directed. How exact or precise are directions, distances, explanations of symbols or hazards, speed, width of road, narrow bridges? How many roads on the left would be passed?

Strip maps were prepared on the duplicator. A group of children were issued with these maps and at a certain predetermined point (detour) the guide explains the alternative direction. Following directions (paper chase) signs and symbols set up to assist travellers to rejoin the main road. Similarly maps were used to direct 'hikers' or 'equestrians' through the area over a different route. Directions to a pilot who may be commissioned to air drop food supplies to a marooned family.

An imaginary island (magimap, magi-story) shows mountains, railways, rivers, highways towns, resources (minerals), products (crops, stock), occupations of people in respective areas (factory, farm).

A study of bridges in the area was made: structure and materials used; different structures over streams, creeks, culverts in depressions.

In the classroom, the children conducted tests on strength of materials by constructing bridges with straws, rolled paper, sticks, string, wool. This led to studying shapes that could give added strength (arches, domes, triangles, squares). Other materials such as wood, paper, plastic and steel were tested for strength. Grouping of samples developed from these tests:

rigid — would not bend
flexible — bend and spring back
plastic — bend and does not spring back

Children constructed a 'swing bridge' between two trees using ropes. At the site children had discussed possibilities of a bridge over a creek being washed away and how a rope swing bridge could be erected across the stream. Another possibility was the felling of a tall tree on the bank of the stream. The skills that had to be considered for this were:

a) estimating the height of the tree
b) how to make the tree fall across the stream from one bank to another
c) how to erect a rope handrail for support

There was an opportunity to visit the army establishment and examine a Bailey bridge; see it constructed and put to use; the strength of the construction and the weight of vehicles that could use it. Discussions led one group to consider methods used by early explorers in crossing flooded streams (floating wagons across, rafts, pontoons). After viewing vehicles on the Bailey bridge, the children looked at the types of tyres of various vehicles: the size of wheels, tread, imprints, number of wheels, caterpillar tracks. From this study, they returned to the site to estimate which vehicles could be permitted to use the road and those which would have to seek an alternative route.

This led the children to look more closely at the road surfaces. Where there had been a washout they could see what materials had been used in previous road constructions and to what depth. From this the children had to consider:

a) maintenance or
b) complete repair and distance of reconstruction

From information collected from the County engineer and Country Roads Board engineer, the children established cubic content of material (metres) and cost. Here they studied economy and contracts. They set up their own tenders and invited contractors to apply. Once again there was written work, reading and spoken activities. Contractors had to convince engineers that materials supplied were suitable for friction to allow vehicles to stop quickly and prevent skidding and bogging.

Safety measures on vehicles were also studied.

The ecology group was interested in road and bridge reconstruction and studied varieties of quick growing materials to help bind materials close to the roadway, allowing a quick run-off of water and eliminating further dangers of erosion.

Experiments with soils and seeds (plants, use of bitumen and wire mesh cover on banks) were studied. As an example, fill a small thin glass jar with seeds, add water until the jar overflows. An airtight lid is then screwed on to the top of the jar. The seeds expand and crack the glass. In breaking the glass, the principle of force and energy in the growing seeds applies to shoots of seeds forcing their way through the bitumen. (Study paved road surfaces.)

Follow-up activities could be done by adding both soil and water to seeds in the jar. Water would need to be constantly added because the soil absorbs the water and there will be some evaporation.

No-one was seriously hurt by the landslide but many local residents had to be evacuated from their homes because of flooding. One group of children decided to find out how these people were assisted and interviewed the helpers concerned with the following issues:

Emergency Groups
   State Relief Committee
   State Emergency Service
   Red Cross
   Search and Rescue
   Army

Local Bodies
   Salvation Army
   Welfare Agencies
   Churches
   Apex
   Rotary
   Lions Club
   St Vincent de Paul

Individuals
   Police
   Doctors

   Ambulance Service
   Storekeepers
   Electricians
   PMG technicians
   Plumbers
   Builders
   Road Construction Workers

Media
   Newspapers and Photographers
   Radio
   Television

The group gathered as much information as possible and then reported back to the whole class. After discussion of the roles played by the helpers, the children broke into groups and improvised many of the aspects of the disaster. Using their understanding of the reality, they were able to develop improvisations that broke away from the usual stereotyped and unimaginative role play so often seen when children are asked to recreate a situation that is outside their own experience.

Some children were concerned with meeting the needs of people who have been injured in an accident. Fortunately no-one had needed medical help this time, but they were very aware of their limited knowledge of first aid. An ambulance officer was invited to give practical demonstrations of the sorts of assistance that should be given at the scene of an accident. He talked about the types of injuries that could be expected and how to deal with them; showed the children supplies and equipment that would be needed; discussed ways in which any injured people could be moved and taken to hospital. He helped the children make a list of essential ite~ for a first aid kit. Children listed possible i- (broken limbs, lacerations, bleeding, sprai posure, shock, suffocation) and worked w.

partner on treating such patients. Because some victims would be unable to walk a stretcher had to be improvised from makeshift materials. Two long saplings were braced together with crosspieces and cords laced across. A blanket was used to soften the base. Tests had to be carried out to make sure the stretcher was safe and strong. The ambulance officer gave advice on how to lift and carry someone without strain on the stretcher bearer.

Members of the Search and Rescue Squad showed ways of performing rescues. Playground equipment was used by the children for rope climbing and rope descent techniques; crossing a horizontal ladder and walking across a log with a rope hand support. Children who had been to the school camp were experienced in the rope assault course, rope swing and flying fox. The Squad members talked about the use of a helicopter and the winch and harness used for rescues in inaccessible areas. Natural supports in the schoolground (trees and a huge stump) were used for anchorage of ropes.

The children in the health group looked at emergency services for food and hygiene in the disaster area and the evacuation site. There were food requirements for different situations:

emergency workers at the disaster area
emergency workers at the evacuation centre
injured people
those who were isolated because of road blockage

The group considered these factors:

a) relationship between the work being done and the food needed
b) the relationships between the physical situation and the amenities available for food preparation
c) the relationships between the injuries sustained by a person and the food required
d) how people were fed in a hospital

The children recorded the following findings: food must have nutritional value; be an energy builder; be light to carry and easily prepared. They visited the local supermarket to see what foods would be suitable, looking at dried and powdered foods and examining packaging for strength. They drew up lists and compared value for money in weights and prices. Although there were farms in the area, certain questions provided much discussion.

What would be better—powdered or fresh milk; fresh or powdered eggs; fresh vegetables or frozen/dried vegetables; tinned or packet soups?

What containers would be used? Weight, durability and ease of carrying were considered.

The availability of water was another consideration. There was no reticulated water supply in the area and tankers would have to take water to the nearest point.

A major health hazard could be the stock in the area. Decisions would have to be made as to whether stock should be transported to other paddocks or left where they were and fodder brought to them. The children had to decide which would be more practicable; what fodder and how much would be required? The local fodder merchant was consulted about the size and weight of a bale of hay; cost, and quantity of hay needed to feed a certain number of stock for a few days.

The problem of disease that could be caused by carcasses was raised. How could these dead stock be quickly removed? Could scavengers like the crow be useful?

The ecology group had been studying ways of moving heavy objects and gave the health group some ideas for the disposal of animals:

a) buried in pits made by the bulldozers
b) piled up and burnt
c) removed by heavy vehicles to a disposal area

This group showed the rest of the class ways and means of moving debris, rocks and trees. They collected smaller objects and improvised levers and rollers were used to pull, push, bump, slide, shift or completely remove the obstacle.

The children decided to re-enact the whole episode of the landslide and divided the school ground into two areas:

the disaster area
the evacuation centre

The story line, characters and action were discussed and the roles allotted. Each group had to understand the coordination of activities for first warnings, rescue operations, transport and reception at the rest centre. Decisions had to be made about injured or trapped persons, whether first aid could be given, the distance from ambulances, and any hazards that could make transportation of the injured a most difficult task. Something had to be arranged for evacuation of all people not actually involved in rescue work. As these problems were discussed and resolved, the children began their role playing.

There were children representing the media in search of 'on the spot' news; 'police' were needed for support and control; workers restoring essential services had to be represented. At the evacuation centre, the roles of emergency groups were established. These involved housing, bedding, clothing, issuing of food and drink; organisation of continuous supplies; arranging 'host' families; rest facilities for exhausted rescue workers; communication with friends and families outside the area. Some children played medical staff and social workers. Many people would be in physical need and others upset emotionally. These people had to be treated and consoled.

Evaluation

At the beginning of the school year the combined teaching staff had developed a school policy emphasising the need for provision of activities to widen the range of individual differences in children as they matured and linking language development, intellectual development and psycho-social development. The school environment had to be dependable and secure so that the children could develop the skills and competencies needed to establish their personal self-esteem.

The evaluation of the *Landslide* theme had to relate to the expressed aims and objectives in the school policy. Much of the evaluation was subjective based on close observation and recording of the children's behaviour, language and social interaction by the teachers involved. This was seen to be valid.

During the theme, development in the social and emotional growth of some pupils, usually reluctant to involve themselves in class activities, was apparent. These children realised they had a contribution to make and became very involved in the project. This was most evident with children who had been reluctant to read and to write. They displayed greater tolerance to others both in the classroom and the playground activities.

The language programme was based on a total approach to listening, speaking, reading and writing. All these were inter-related and inter-dependent. Direct experiences were important for spoken language activities incorporating sensory and drama activities. They were the source for the children's language programme.

Written Activities From The Landslide *Theme*

1 Note taking, particularly in summary form, which was then arranged in logical sequence into final report form.
2 Pre-planning, indicating detailed outlines of activities to be followed and types of questions to be used for inquiry purposes.
3 Writing notices to parents and local authorities, and preparing invitations for speakers to visit the school.
4 Writing letters, which required some study of formal letter presentation. Children learned skills of setting out, heading, address, salutation. They decided on the content and made sure all information was included for the reader's complete understanding. They also learned the convention of correctly addressing envelopes.
5 Map drawing; writing directions for others to read and follow on maps; understanding signs and symbols commonly used.
6 Using photographs and illustrations for:
  a) dictionary work-picture and explanation or meaning; children developed dictionaries about the theme;
  b) language experience approach to reading. A sentence or paragraph was written under a picture. Many of these sentences were transcribed from the cassettes used in interviews. The actual language of the children and the person being interviewed was matched with the photographs or illustrations.
7 Writing classified advertisements (for sale, lost and found, equipment, auctions, country properties, remedies, community meetings).
8 Writing reports for the local paper. Children studied journalists' reports and wrote their own versions. They also drew up their own rainfall records, river heights, stock reports and weather maps.
9 Writing an agenda for a council meeting.
10 Drawing up ballot papers for voting.
11 Writing posters and public notices (warnings, trespassers).
12 Devising requisition forms for clothing, furniture.
13 Treasure maps, magi-maps and magi-tales. Magi-maps are similar to treasure maps which can be drawn on greaseproof paper and burnt around the edges with a candle to give an ancient parchment effect. Such maps can be in a variety of shapes incorporating numerous signs, symbols or features. By using this map and introducing characters, an imaginative story can be compiled. Hence children construct a 'magi-map' and write a 'magi-tale'. Such a tale is most effective for drama activities and if cameras are used the whole tale is captured in pictorial form and an interesting language experience can be compiled in a photograph album and ultimately housed in the school library.
14 Reports on discovery in problem solving, science and mathematics.
15 Recipe writing.
16 First aid requirements and instructions.
17 Poems.
18 News and radio bulletins.
19 Creative story telling and writing. Children used the overhead projector and class chalkboard.
20 Inventors. Children were asked to invent something that would assist in the following areas:
  a) accommodation (inflatable houses)
  b) transport (a vehicle performing a number of tasks at one time)
  c) bridge construction
  d) an avalanche detector or preventer

From the huge amount of written work presented by the children, teachers had a great opportunity to help children evaluate their own writing. The purposes for writing were so diverse that children had to develop a variety of styles and presentation of content. The appropriateness of the style to the content became very important to the children.

Assistance was given to individual children's writing. If there were many errors the teacher noted these but only treated one aspect at that time. Errors noted but not treated immediately became part of general continued instruction. If a number of children shared a similar weakness they were given specific instruction and reinforcement material was then used for consolidation. If children had spelling problems often they were also weak readers, so a word study programme was set up by the teacher to help eliminate the problems. In word attack, blends caused the major concern so sequence work was planned — *s, sc, scr.*

Word games were then used extensively to maintain interest in words; origins and history of words, antonymns, synonymns, homonymns, prefixes, suffixes, base words were all incorporated.

Vocabulary charts were compiled by the pupils from the theme and each child also compiled an individual thesaurus plus a section for individual word lists. A variety of dictionaries, from the picture type to *Oxford Junior* and *Roget's Thesaurus,* were available in the room.

Visual and auditory perception improved and greater use was made of the other senses.

As the school had no library, a store room was converted into a resource room which held projectors, cassette recorders, radio, television set, listening posts, overhead projector, pictures, charts, film strips, slides and books.

The books were arranged into these groups:
a) sequential readers
b) interest readers
c) leisure reading

Interest readers were divided into two areas (easy reading and more difficult reading) and were used when a child was following a theme or interest. If the child had problems with reading the teacher 'taught' that aspect to the child with reinforcement by use of aids and sequential readers. Comprehension was done at different levels using listening posts, readers or laboratories, ensuring that literal, interpretative, critical and creative comprehension skills were being used.

There were no specialist teachers on the staff so the teachers shared their own expertise in music, physical education, drama, art and craft.

Aesthetics were apparent in presentation of material and room arrangement and decoration.

Drama outdoors

Listening – Individual
Children sit in a close group and listen to sounds in the environment. They listen for sounds nearby and those that are further away. Give them time to concentrate and identify the sounds. Ask them to locate sounds that are natural to the environment and those that are not. They should try to find and identify four separate sounds. Then ask these questions:

Do you notice any sounds that surprise you?
How do the sounds make you feel?

Ask the children to sit still for three minutes (it will seem a very long time). They close their eyes and 'soak in' the sounds around them. When the three minutes are over, they turn to someone nearby and express their feelings.

Listening – With A Partner
The children sit close to their partner and whisper secret sounds and messages. They can have friendly whispers, fierce whispers and mysterious whispers. Ask them to make up a funny whispering language.

Calling Out Across Distances
1 Partners separate but stay within sight of one another. They experiment to find out which vocal sound carries best (try calling 'coo-ee').
2 Partner **A** calls out instructions for partner **B** to follow. **B** keeps moving further away until **A** can no longer be heard.
3 Partner **A** stands about three metres away from **B**. **A** closes eyes and is called over to **B**. **B** can use normal words or make special sounds for **A** to follow. Partners reverse the roles.
4 Partners stand close together. **A** is blindfolded and is talked around an obstacle course by **B**. For example, around trees, over logs. **B** walks beside **A** giving vocal guidance.

Listening – Small Groups
1 The children can use a tape recorder to make a sound story. They record sounds in the environment and then make them into a story with a linking narrative.
2 One child acts as an interviewer and interviews other group members. They give their impressions of the sounds they have heard around them.

Listening – Whole Group
The whole group forms a large circle. Each child creates an individual sound; all close their eyes and each one tries to walk across to the opposite side of the circle.

They make their sounds continuously as a warning signal to others and try not to touch one another.

Rhythm Work – Whole Group
Circle formation again. One child is selected as leader. The leader claps a rhythm pattern and the group repeats it. The leader tries different patterns with the group echoing them.

The leader then selects one pattern and claps it, slaps knees in rhythm; group repeats this. Then the leader invents a chant to go with the rhythm and starts again—claps, slaps knees, waves hands, nods head, chanting in rhythm all the time. All the children follow the pattern with the leader. The whole group finishes up chanting, clapping, waving, nodding, stamping and moving around quite freely without bumping.

Change the leader and vary the sound of the chant and the pace of the movement by suggesting moods *friendly, fierce, sad, happy.*

Looking – Individual

Ask the children to begin looking up as they walk; noticing the sky, clouds, treetops, tops of buildings, birds. They then look down for a while and notice the surface on which they are walking. Examine it for texture, kinds of surface, edges, feel. Now they walk very quickly and finish up running. Ask them:

Does speed alter the way you see things?
Stroll around very, very slowly; wandering around and about. What do you see now?
Look at trees, rocks, earth and grass from different angles. Do the trees look different if you lie flat on your back to watch them?
How does a rock look if you press your nose up against it?

The children should notice the light qualities of areas and how they change; standing still and looking around:

What colours take your eye?
What building attracts you?
What movement do you notice?

Looking – With A Partner

Pair the children and direct them in the following activities:

Choose a large green park or open space and enter it with your partner. Stop somewhere and look around. Take notice of the design of this open space and discuss how this design is affecting the use of the space. Have you any ideas of alternative ways of designing the space?

Find something in the area that really interests you and take your partner to it. Point out all the interesting things about it and discuss it with your partner. Let your partner find something to show you.

Look at the sky and try your skill as a weather forecaster. There may be other features in the environment that will help you to predict the weather. Your partner can try changing your comments into the more formal presentation of a television commentator.

When you are looking at the local shopping area, choose an object in one of the shop windows and become that object. See how it feels and stay as that object for a while. Can your partner guess which object you are?

As you look you may see things you would like to change and some you would leave as they are. Discuss this with your partner.

Let your partner walk ahead and you follow. Copy your partner's way of walking and see if you can feel the way your partner is feeling. The two of you may plan a sequence when the first person becomes another personality (an outstanding athlete).

Make a trail for your partner to follow. Use tracking signs and specially written messages. You could even make a treasure map.

Looking – With Small Groups

In this activity the children search for an area of housing. They look at the houses and 'read' them to others in the group. Everybody helps to 'read' the houses as places people look after in their own ways. The children can discuss the ways the gardens are set out; how the houses are painted and decorated and what sort of people live there.

They should look at the buildings in a street. Draw quick sketches to show them next to one another; show whether they are big or small, ugly or pretty, quiet or loud, wide or narrow. Discuss whether the houses suit one another the way they are designed and placed. Does the street look boring or interesting?

Looking – With Whole Group

Shadowing Game

All the children move around, at a walking pace, in a given area. Each child chooses another to shadow. The shadower must try not to be noticed. Players challenge anyone they think is shadowing them. The shadower is 'out' if identified. Continue until nearly all are caught.

Touching – With A Partner

☐ Sit back to back with your partner. Try to communicate feelings through this body contact.

☐ **Imagine your partner is a fossil embedded in earth and rock for millions of years and you are a geologist working with hammer, chisel and brush to free the fossil from the surrounding earth.**

☐ Decide on some object in the environment (tree, bush, rock, stump) into which your partner can be changed. Close your eyes and physically mould your partner into this shape. When you are satisfied, open your eyes to check. Your partner then tries to guess which object is represented.

Smelling

Ask the children to stop still for a few moments and breathe deeply (inhaling through the nose and exhaling fully through an open mouth several times).

What is the smell of the environment?

Is it pleasant?

Can something be identified just by its smell?

Movement And Sound – Whole Group

Use a tambourine as an accompaniment to the children's movement and also as a stopping signal. Children find their own place in a given area. They move freely but are not allowed to make body contact with any other child.

☐ To the tambourine accompaniment, the children rise from the ground and stretch their bodies as high and as wide as possible. On a sharp signal, they collapse on the ground; letting their breath go in a rush at the same time.

☐ Repeat, but slow down the collapse with a slow shaking of the tambourine. Wait until the last child is on the ground before the sound stops. Let the children sigh 'aaahh!' as their breath is expelled.

☐ All the children crouch low to the ground. Make a slow drumming on the tambourine. Slowly they grow to make a large expansive shape. They start humming as they grow and when growth is nearly complete change humming to a full-throated 'aaahh!' The growth can be towards a number of different shapes or the weight and balance can be on one body part. For example,

61

the hip, and movement can emphasise this part of the body.

- ☐ The children take their bodies into available areas as other children move around them. Each child's body is adapted to the space available and they reach out as far as they can at all levels.

Story Writing – With Small Groups

Each group is given an outline of a story and develops it in their own way. Discuss certain aspects the children might consider:

A group of people have to make a journey through unknown country.

The children are asked to consider the following:

a) What is the purpose of the journey?

b) What could be the possible dangers?

c) List all those involved, people and animals.

d) Do they expect trouble and danger?

e) Have they any friends nearby who could help them?

f) Is the country hostile?

g) If so, is it because of its nature or inhabitants?

h) Give some outline of the people involved; what do they look like; how old are they; what sort of personalities do they have; have they any special abilities or needs; what are their names?

i) Where is the journey taking place?

Discuss these points with the whole class and then circulate amongst the small groups raising these issues and any other possible extensions to the children's developing story line. The children will have to make decisions as to the difficulties the travellers have to face and how they will overcome or succumb to these trials. It is up to them to decide whether it will be a story of triumph or failure.

Story Writing – Individual

Children are given the beginning of a story and have to write their own ending. This could provide a story line for a later improvisation.

I had established camp beside the creek and had been there for nearly two days. It was early evening and there was a curious stillness in the air. As I lay on the grassy patch beside my tent I could see the first stars, pale in the darkening sky. The birds had quietened and all was peaceful. As I looked at the sky I saw a strange brighter star. It moved across the sky, coming closer and closer. It was travelling at a fantastic pace. The light grew blindingly bright and I could see a definite shape. This hovered over my camp and then drifted slowly northward as if looking for a place to land. It descended behind the nearby pine trees and I was irresistibly drawn to follow it . . .

Improvisations

Divide the class into four groups. Each group is to be responsible for representing one of the four seasons and must decide how to depict this. They may look at the plant life, bird life, animal life, reactions of humans to the elements, music and song associated with the season.

NARRATIVE STORY

In this activity all the children work simultaneously. Provide the narrative and the children interpret it individually as they follow the story line.

You are out in the bush walking across a paddock—the ground is lumpy and uneven and you have to be careful not to twist your ankles—look carefully. It is very slippery because of the rain and the grasses squash and slip beneath your feet. Your shoes are getting muddy and as you walk the mud grows heavier; your legs feel heavy. Pick your way across the field; sometimes with long strides, sometimes with little hopping steps. There is a smell of mushrooms in the paddock, sniff the air and smell them. Search for them amongst the grasses; the little button ones just peeping through the soil and the great dark brown flat ones. Can you tell how old a mushroom is?

The animals have been in the paddock. You can see their droppings; the small black balls that the sheep drop and the great flat cakes of manure from the cows. Some country people used fresh hot manure as a poultice for chilblains. What do you think of that for a cure? Many country people used materials close at hand for home remedies.

Across the paddock you see a large black horned animal that looks suspiciously like a bull; really very much like a bull. Yes, very, very much like a bull.

(Use percussion background)

Quicken your stride but try not to draw attention to yourself. There is no need to panic. Look over your shoulder; yes, he is definitely showing signs of interest. A little quicker, look again; he is pawing at the ground and making snorting sounds. The breath from his nostrils is steamy in the cold air. Quicker, quicker—don't panic—your own breath is steaming out; your chest is heaving up and down; you can hear your panting breath. Your legs and arms move like pistons, up and down, up and down; faster, faster, the fence is near. Look again the fence is near. OK, but so is the bull. Run for your life run! Run! Run! Here is the fence, scramble through. Quickly! Quickly! Don't get caught! You're through. Oh! you're through! Here is the bull. Who's afraid of the bull? It's only a poor old cow. Get your breath back; take it easy, rest, rest. Try to relax. Rub your tired legs. Your socks are covered in prickly burrs. Try and pull them off before they scratch the skin. That was close, wasn't it?

Walk across this paddock. You are rather tired after your adventure, take it easy. There's a bit of a creek running through here. There is a pile of stones—water worn pebbles—smooth and glistening when wet. See if you can throw stones across the creek. Pick up a very large heavy rock; really large, feel the weight in your hands. Now slowly lift it and raise it above your head, arms back and heave it into the middle of the creek. Watch the splash; watch all the rings of water from the middle of the pool right to the very edges. Stand still and quiet and watch.

At your feet you see a very unusual stone. It has strange colours; pick it up and rub the mud off it. Wash it and rub it dry on your jumper. As you rub the stone you feel yourself beginning to turn around and around and as you turn around you feel yourself becoming larger and larger until you grow into a great giant.

(Sound with tambourine or cymbal for slow growing climax will help both turning around and growing. A clear end to the climax of sound helps control)

You take great strides stretching your legs as you walk over the countryside.

(Long measured time beats)

But there are dead trees in your way. Using all your strength, pull out the trees by their roots and throw them away. Look down at things from your great height; stretch your great arms; your fierce crushing fingers; your big flat feet. Stamp along. When you look down again you find that you have come around in a full circle—people do this sometimes when they are lost in the bush—you are back at the pool. You see another strange stone. Pick it up, rub it on your jumper; you become a very small bird, a baby bird who can't even fly. Hop around for a bit. What are these strange things sticking out from your body? Flap them about for a while—why I think they're wings. Practise using them. Gradually you get better at using them and you are able to soar off into the sky.

(Again a slow rolling climax of sound for practice in using wings and then fly off, then with up and down rolling rhythms. The bird is helped to fly and a slow de-climax finally brings it back to earth)

The bird finds itself back at the pool. It picks up another stone and starts to rub off the mud. It finds itself turning around and around and growing thin and tall and stiff; growing into a puppet.

(Use percussion background again)

The puppet enjoys dancing by the pool.

(Gay rhythm for dancing)

The puppet becomes stiff and sharp and as it dances its sharp feet get stuck in the mud until it cannot move any more.

(Use rhythm. Slow it down to help experience of standing in mud and getting more and more stuck. Use one final loud sound on the tambourine when puppet cannot move anymore)

The puppet looks down at the mud and sees a green stone; bends down very stiffly and starts to rub it. Slowly the puppet begins to turn and turn until finally the puppet is changed back into being you.

You are are very tired after your adventures, so walk back slowly through the paddocks. Back through the fence; the cow has gone to the milking shed. Slowly, slowly you are so tired. Now you are back; lie down and rest.

Games

Traditional games were characterised by simplicity, spontaneity and total involvement. They were filled with cooperation, fun and laughter. When there was competition there was also compassion. The players controlled the competition, it did not control them. The games had four basic components:

cooperation
involvement
acceptance
fun

Play some of these games with your children. Even older primary children get a lot of fun out of games like. *What's the Time, Mr Wolf?; Who Goes Round My House Tonight?; Twos and Threes; Drop the Hanky.* You can update them or use them as the basis of a new game created by you and the children.

Every game you have ever played can be varied to create new games; just remember that the games design should match the social and emotional developmental stages of the children with whom you are working. Ask the children to help design games—it's a real intellectual exercise.

Cooperative Musical Chairs
This is a variation of the original. The original version is a great game, but if twenty children play there must be nineteen losers. In this new game the object is to keep every child in the game even though the chairs are being removed. As each chair is removed, more children have to team together sitting on parts of chairs or parts of one another to keep everyone in the game. Instead of fighting for sole possession of one chair, the children work together to make themselves part of it.

Collective Games
These vary traditional games by having two or more teams working towards a common end. One team does not achieve its success by competing against another or at the expense of another, but rather as a result of working together with the other team.

Collective Score Blanket Ball
Two teams attempt to toss a beach ball over a volley ball net using only a blanket. Everytime the ball is blanket-tossed over the net by one team and successfully blanket-caught by the other team, one collective point is scored.

Reversal Games
Vary our traditional concept of teams winning and losing. In some cases points are given to the other team and scorers switched, and in most cases players become members of both teams. Once you get used to such a revolutionary idea, you will find lots of games to reverse. The following game is an example.

Rotational Volley Ball
Instead of rotating within the opposite teams, the rotation of players includes both teams. Once a server from both teams has relinquished the service, they move to the middle of the back line of the *other* team. It is difficult to get mad at the other team or to lose to the other team as you will become part of the other team.

Non-Sexist Volley Ball

Start with boys on one side of the net and girls on the other. Whenever a person on one team hits the ball over the net she or he scoots under the net to the other side. The objective is to make a complete change in teams with as few drops of the ball as possible. Boys and girls will be happily integrated.

Obstacle People

Children form into single file groups. The first player's body is used to form an obstacle. The second player has to get past the obstacle. Then the second player's body becomes an obstacle. It can join onto the first obstacle or separate. The following players continue the game until they are all obstacles. It is interesting to see how creative the children can be in the flexible use of their bodies.

Obstacle Course

Set up an obstacle course of varied types of materials that will allow jumping over, crawling under, getting through activities. There will be no racing as this game is designed for individuals to go through the course at their own pace. Time each one from start to finish with a stopwatch. Now ask the children to go through the course again exactly duplicating their own times. Once the technique is known, divide the children into groups and let each group appoint a leader to use the stopwatch.

Variation On Obstacle Course

Each child has a partner giving verbal advice and directions through the obstacle course. Partner **A** will be blindfolded and taken through the course by sighted partner **B**. **B** will have to use very specific language to successfully guide **A** and there will be a fair amount of body contact as **A** is manipulated through the obstacle course. Encourage this language, particularly the use of prepositions *under*, *above, through, next to, on, beneath* and the use of adverbs *slowly, easily, quickly*.

Octopus

The playing area is a marked square. The players (the fish) stand side by side on one edge of the square. There are three octopuses in the centre of the square. When the leader calls 'octopus', the fish have to try to reach the other side without being touched by the octopuses. If the fish are touched they must sit on their bottoms and dangle their feet and hands hoping to touch a fish. When the remaining fish are lined up on the opposite side, the leader again calls 'octopus' and the game continues until all are octopuses.

Tangle Touch

This is a circle game with six to twelve players. They stand in a close circle with sides touching and both hands stretched out towards the middle of the circle. Each player grasps somebody's hand on the opposite side, being sure not to grab the same person's hand twice. The group then have to try and untangle themselves into one or two circles by exchanging places, following arms, swapping sides or twisting under or over arms. This will cause a great deal of discussion as the group sets itself to solve the problems.

Radar

Children work with a partner. They decide on a sound and practise making the sound together. Partner **A** has closed eyes and partner **B** starts to move away making the sound. **A** follows the sound. **B** should not get too far away—about a metre would be the maximum length. **B** has to lead only by sound and must also guard **A** from bumping into any of the other children. Reverse partners.

Chain Tag

One pair of players is chosen to be 'it'. They join hands and chase the others. Each player that is tagged joins up until they are all chained together. Only the players at each end of the chain may tag another.

Environmental Tag

This is a game of speed and ecological knowledge. The game planner lays out a course about 500 metres long. Starting at home base, players are taken on a nature walk along the course during which they are told the names of ten to fifteen flowers, trees, plants or rocks. At the far end of the course certain players are appointed 'it'. There should be one 'it' for every five to ten players. The object of the game is to get back to home base without being tagged by 'it'. Players are safe whenever they are touching one of the identified plants. 'It' may challenge players to name the plant they are touching. If they cannot remember the name or give the wrong one they are considered to be caught and are out of the game. 'It' may also tag players in the normal way when they are not touching identified plants. All those who reach home base win.

It is important to stress the care of the environment. The children when chasing must be careful not to damage the area, and the children touching the plant must do so gently.

Musical Chairs

Children form a circle and the music starts. In the centre is a line of chairs, one less than the number of children. When the music stops each child has to find a chair. The game continues until there is only one chair left. Those who miss a chair clap along with the music.

Pass The Balloons

Children stand in a circle. Several have a long balloon between their knees. They have to pass the balloons to the child next to them using only their knees. When the music stops, the players with the balloons are 'out'. If they burst a balloon they are also 'out'.

Lifebelts

Similar to musical chairs; when the music or clapping stops the players must rush for a lifebelt. These can be represented by chalk circles drawn on the floor or the wall. When they touch the lifebelt they are not allowed to touch each other. Each time the music or clapping starts again a lifebelt is covered up. The idea is to see how many children who are left to touch the last lifebelt can do it without touching another child.

Number Play

The children form a circle and keep moving in time to the music. When the music stops the leader calls out a number and the children have to form a group of that number. Those who cannot are 'out' and help clap time with the music. The game continues until only two or three children are left.

Guess The Environment

Divide the class into groups. Each group chooses two players who leave the group and discuss *who* they are and *where* they are going to be. They return to the group who have to guess from the pair's actions in the environment and their general discussion just *who* they are and *where* they are. The mystery pair may have a very generalised discussion that gives very few clues as to *who* but their actions could be more specific to indicate *where*. For example, a pair of goldminers could talk about the weather but their actions would be chipping rocks, digging sand and gravel and washing the sand in the creek.

Drawing The Object

Divide the children into two teams, each with a leader. The leader is placed about two metres from the team. Each leader has a prepared list of objects. Each team sends a player to the leader who shows both players the same word. (If the children are non-readers the leader whispers the word to each player.) They run back to their teams and on large sheets of paper they draw the object so that their team mates can identify it. The first team to call out the object correctly wins a point; if a team calls out an object incorrectly they lose a point. Continue with two new players until each team member has had a chance to draw an object. This is not a guessing game. As the children become more experienced they should be able to focus on some element of the object that can be quickly recognised by the group. With older children use abstract words like *strength, joy, triumph, sorrow.* Let the children make up a list of objects for you to give the leader. These could relate to a recent excursion or a studied theme.

Tug Of War

Have two long lines of children each four metres from the rope. When both sides are ready they run in and pick up the rope and pull in opposite directions. The referee stands in the middle.

Crows And Cranes

Two teams face each other, one team is the 'crows' and the other team 'cranes'. A home base is marked by drawing a straight line about ten metres behind each team. Once they run over this line they are safe. The referee calls out 'crr. . . crr. . . crows' or 'crr. . . crr. . . cranes'. The side whose name is called runs for the home base, while the other team chases them and tries to catch as many as they can before they reach safety. A captured player must join the other side. Ask the children for other combinations. For example, dogs and donkeys, koalas and kangaroos; frogs and ferrets.

Ned Kelly 1, 2, 3

Have three players in the middle of the playing area. On the call 'Ned Kelly 1, 2, 3' the other players must try to reach the opposite end of the area. If the players in the centre can lift one of the runners off the ground long enough to call out 'Ned Kelly 1, 2, 3' that runner becomes one of the centre team. The game continues until everyone is in the centre.

Variation

Instead of lifting players off the ground, players have to be tagged long enough to say 'Ned Kelly 1, 2, 3'.

Find The Match

Have two sets of cards; one set has pictures of animals, fish, birds, reptiles the other set has the names of the animals. Provide exactly the same number of cards as there are players. Shuffle the cards and let each child choose one. Without speaking the children get on their knees and make the sound and action of their card. The partners have to find their match but they must not talk. When they think they have found their partner they must stop moving and wait for a referee to check their cards. They can then leave the game. Vary the cards to suit the theme on which the children are working.

Snake In The Grass

Choose a child to play 'snake'. While 'snake' lies on the ground sleeping in the sun, the other children creep up and gently touch him/her. When the leader claps hands and the 'snake' wakes up, anyone touched by the 'snake' lies down and also becomes a 'snake'. The other children run amongst the 'snakes' teasing them and seeing how close they can get without being caught. The game continues until everyone is tagged and you have the ground covered with wriggling 'snakes'.

Growth Experiences

Everyone is blindfolded or eyes shut and is standing apart in the room. They then slowly move around and shake hands with everyone they come in contact with. After a time everyone can join hands with the people they touch so that one or more circles should be formed.

Variation 1

Everyone with eyes shut. They start to move making vocal sounds, touching everyone they come in contact with. Each child tries to find someone making a similar sound. Eyes are kept closed.

Variation 2

The group chooses a word to say, *bananas, zipper, troll*. Everyone closes eyes and starts to move while repeating the word. When they come into contact with someone they say the word in a certain mood—menacingly, friendly, lovingly, angrily, sadly, excitedly. The group continues on, conveying a different mood the next time they meet someone.

Animal Images

The children decide on the animals they will become and start to move as that animal, exploring levels, directions, speeds and quality of movement, as well as how certain body parts would move. For example, spine, back legs, neck, head, tail. Sound is then added—the appropriate sounds the animals make while moving in certain situations and surroundings. Animals then become humans again but still retain the animal qualities. For example, stealth, tension, awareness and, if speaking, using the quality of animal sound in their voices.

Listen For The Sound

The children form a large circle, sitting cross-legged with their heads down and eyes closed. They are asked to think of all the sounds that can be made with their mouths, hands and bodies. When the teacher stops talking they sit for a few seconds to listen to any sounds being made in the room. After a few more seconds anyone in the circle can start a particular sound. Everyone else begins to repeat the sound so that the whole circle is making the same sound. After a while someone else in the circle should change to a new sound and again the whole circle repeats the sound. Look for variety.

Guess Who Starts The Sound

Divide the class into groups of about ten to twelve. Each group chooses someone to leave the room while they decide who will be the 'sound starter'. They practise with the 'sound starter' so that their synchronisation is very close and then the 'guesser' is brought back into the room. The 'sound starter' and the group can change the sounds to make it difficult for the 'guesser' to tell who is leading the group. Allow three guesses and then change both leader and guesser. The whole group must cooperate if the leader is to remain unknown.

Variation

Instead of sounds the children could initiate movements. This is probably easier to detect as the children in the group will have to watch for the movement change and their eyes may give them away.

Serial Story

Children sit in a circle and one player is chosen to begin the story. It could be an improvised story or a re-telling of an old favourite. At any time the teacher can point to another player who must continue exactly where the last player stopped. Players must continue without repeating the last word the previous player spoke. Try to keep the storyline flowing with all players involved and intent on the narrator. If the players can develop the story and bring it to a climax then all will have a feeling of success. This game presupposes that the class teacher has told the children many stories and they have acquired some story telling skills and a sense of form. Use a tape recorder or take brief notes of the children's stories so that they can be typed up for children to read later.

Music Story Using Rhythm And Melody

The first player starts to hum or sing a made up tune. At any point he/she can indicate another player who must immediately continue the tune.

Variation 1

At any time after the leader starts, any member of the group can break in and continue. As soon as this happens, the leader must stop singing.

Variation 2

The leader starts humming or singing. Other members of the group can join in at any time with the leader. All keep singing, trying to get blending harmonies or chords.

These variations can be used by one group to accompany another group's verbal story telling. This would involve a great deal of cooperation and work between the groups as the coordination would need to be perfect. A third group could become involved in coordinating sound effects and a fourth group would provide visual effects. Encourage the children to work towards a cooperative project like this.

Building A Story

Using the whole class, have each child write five or six familiar words on cards or pieces of paper. They put their names or initials on the backs of the card in order to collect them later, either for future playing or to add to their personal word collection.

Form teams of three to five children. The group chooses a leader who spreads out his/her collection of word cards so that all the group can see. They then work together, arranging and re-arranging the word cards to build a story. If connecting words are needed the players write them on new cards or slips of paper and place them in context. When the story is completed the first player writes it out in the group story book and keeps the original words and the new words for his/her own collection. The next player then spreads out collected words and the group again tries to build a story. This is a useful game for children who are using *Breakthrough to Literacy*. As children become used to this story form, they could put all the cards together and see if they could build a story from everyone's words.

Make a space box

Find a strong cardboard box with a lid; a shoebox would be about the size you need. You will need scissors, tape, felt pens and paper. Make a small peephole in one end of the box and then cut a square hole in the lid away from the peephole.

Cover the hole in the lid with some paper to filter the light. You can use coloured tissue, cellophane, greaseproof paper, *Gladwrap,* or aluminium foil with a few holes in it for the light to penetrate the dark places in the box. Hold the paper in place with sticky tape. Put the lid aside and see if you can build an environment in your box. Line the sides and back of the box with something to make a background. Look for magazines with pictures you could use (buildings and streets for city environments; hills and clouds for country environments). You might find some interesting colours and textures in fabrics and silver foil with shiny black paper makes effective patterns or a night sky.

Make the bottom of the box the ground. You can use sand or pebbles, plastic grass, tinsel or a small piece of carpet. Use mirror pieces for water. Plastic straws can make electricity poles and you could use nylon fishing line for telegraph wires. Collect cut out figures, trees and buildings from the magazines. Tape small pieces of card to the backs of your cut outs and then tape them into position. Keep looking at them through the peephole to see where they should go. If you want things to hang down into the box tape them on fine cotton and stick them to the underside of the lid.

Hold your space box under a strong light or use a torch and look through the peephole. You have made another world. Share the boxes amongst the class and see how many different ways there are to make an environment.

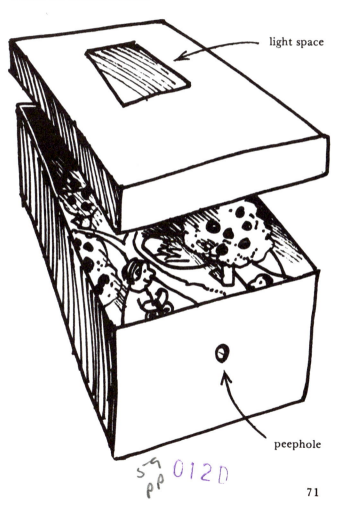

light space

peephole

71